P9-CCX-346

****
*
* The Cool Parents' Guide to All of New York
*
****

The Cool Parents' Guide to All of New York:

Excursions and Activities In and Around

Our City that Your Children Will Love and

You Won't Think Are Too Bad Either

****

THIRD EDITION

****

Alfred Gingold and Helen Rogan

****

UNIVERSE * NEW YORK

This book is for Toby, cool kid par excellence.

First Universe edition published in the United States of America in 2003
by UNIVERSE PUBLISHING
a Division of Rizzoli International Publications, Inc.
300 Park Avenue South
New York, NY 10010
www.rizzoliUSA.com

Previously published by City and Company
Interior Design by Don Wise & Co., based on an original design by Nancy Steiny
Cover Design: Paul Kepple and Jude Buffum @ Headcase Design
Cover Illustration by Mary Lynn Blasutta

2007 / 10 9 8 7 6 5

Printed in the United States
Library of Congress Catalog Control Number: 2002111641

ISBN-13:978-0-7893-0857-3

Preface

Much has changed since the first edition of this book appeared in 1996. The dancing chicken of Chinatown has gone to her reward and the Police Museum has moved twice. MoMA has temporarily migrated to Queens, which has become the new Brooklyn, which has become the new Manhattan, which still contains the city's most popular attractions. The city's most visited site these days is one you might hesitate to show your children: it is the site of the World Trade Center.

In many ways, though, New York is the same. It still crackles with a vitality that few cities on earth can match and it still holds surprises, excitements and pleasures that not even the most jaded, been-there-done-that New Yorkers can resist—and that goes for their kids as well.

To prepare this new edition, we've revisited our old favorites and introduced some new ones. And of course, we've had help. Our thanks to Bronwyn Prohaska, Holly Rothman, and Helene Silver.

—A. G. & H. R.

Table of Contents

Chapter One
Into the Melting Pot: Ethnic New York

Chapter Two
Museums: New Ways to Look at Old Things

Chapter Three
The City's Best-kept Secrets (Right Under Your Nose)

Chapter Four
Cityscapes: All Around the Town

What Is a Cool Parent?

A cool parent is one who does not view family activities intended for the child's enrichment as a vale of unrelenting boredom, typified by trips to diddly museums where some unemployed actress in a mobcap tells you about beeswax. No sirree. The cool parent has higher aspirations involving enjoyment, pleasure, fun.

Unfortunately, the cool parent in the quest for quality time doesn't get much help from newspapers and magazines. Children's listings tend to be arid, devoid of nitty-gritty: an address, a phone number, hours of operation, not much more. New Yorkers need to know more, and much more, before they set out toward parts unknown or even parts beyond their building. Sure, the Queens Museum sounds interesting, but how do you get there, and what do you aim for once inside? (Answer: a 40-minute subway ride from Times Square and the Panorama of the City of New York.) Is it easy to get from there to the legendary Pearson's Texas Barbecue for barbecue? (It is.)

This book addresses the reality of being a (cool) New York City parent: discriminating, inquisitive, pressed for time, wanting to know there will be decent food nearby, and, above all, that children and parents alike will have a good time. Everybody knows how much there is to do in our city. What New York parents need is a little help finding the best of both the familiar and the offbeat.

To that end, *The Cool Parents' Guide* offers a series of day trips, clusters of activities and sights, with enough variety and leeway within each of them to keep everybody happy. We tell you what to expect, where you can eat, and what else there is to see or do in the vicinity.

There are few children's museums in this book. Sure, they can be great for the kids, and you'll certainly visit your fair share of them before your parenting days are through; but no one in his or her right mind would claim children's museums are fun for adults. Likewise, we do not dwell on attractions that seem to us already well-known and utilized by New Yorkers, such as Central Park—which, if you haven't already visited, you really should. As devoted New Yorkers and parents ourselves, we guarantee all information for up-to-the-minute (but not beyond) accuracy and attitude.

So all you really need to decide is whether or not you are cool. Read our manifesto and see if you match the profile.

The Cool Parents' Manifesto

1. The cool parent demands the right, if only *in principle*, to enjoy family excursions, while acknowledging that this is not always possible (unless you're mad for cartoons or miniature golf). For some parents, coolness means never going to Disney-anything. So be it. (Although sometimes you do have to.)

2. The cool parent is mindful of the strategic importance of a cab, remembering the consequences of arriving at the appointed destination with kids already bored, exhausted, or whining.

3. To those who would persuade the cool parent to bring the whole gang to a mask-making workshop, we say: We'll get back to you.

4. Ditziness can be attractive in the young, but the cool parent always phones ahead for details, schedules, admission prices, and directions. The cool parent consults a detailed map *before* starting out. (That's why we've included some.) *Then the cool parent brings the map along!*

5. The cool parent always carries snacks, aware that kids have to eat when they have to eat and that gnawing hunger can mess up an outing before it's begun.

6. Speaking of food, the cool parent understands that there's more to family dining-out than McDonald's, Wendy's, and the local pizza joint.

7. The cool parent shuns like the plague parades, street fairs, food festivals, and the like for any child under the age of ten. Here's why:

* Little kids at these functions are routinely stepped on and elbowed.

* The noise and the crush is so great that you can't even hear what's wrong when your wailing child tugs at your arm and tries to tell you.

* Nothing could interest a child less than stained-glass doodads and foods of many lands.

* Brass bands, bagpipers, and steel drummers terrify them.

8. The cool parent is aware that at regular intervals the kids will need to "veg out," that is, to give up on meaningful activity and watch TV or do something equally moronic. Those inclined to guilt can make an enriching experience out of this, such as a Buster Keaton film festival with different kinds of homemade popcorn and other treats. You could even forget the homemade aspect.

9. The cool parent is an improvisational virtuoso. (By which we mean, if something isn't working, bag it.)

10. The cool parent knows that discretion is the better part of valor, and that, in New York, it always pays to keep your eyes open, especially in unfamiliar territory. But the cool parent is not a scaredy-cat, even when venturing into terra incognita (say, down a manhole in the middle of Atlantic Avenue, see page 56).

Is this you? Of course it is. As a New York City parent, you're already cooler than most, since New York City is the world's coolest place (and remember, our great city includes boroughs that are not Manhattan). We know that you're perennially up for the treasures, excitements, serendipities, and secrets that New York has to offer—except, of course, when it feels like a better day to stay home and lurk around, which is also a very cool thing to do.

How to Use This Book

Like Dr. Scholl's moleskin, these excursions should be trimmed to fit. Many of them include more than you and yours will be able to cover in one day. Our aim is not to exhaust you, but to provide frameworks within which you can create your own itineraries, depending on the ages, interests, and energy levels of your kids.

We live in a rapidly changing world, and nothing changes more often or arbitrarily than business hours. So we've simply provided all the necessary phone numbers. Trust no one but the horse's (or museum's) mouth. **CALL AHEAD FIRST.** (Another good reason to do so is to find out about additional programs and special events. Many of the institutions we recommend offer children's programs in everything from kite-flying to map-making. So go on, call.) All phone numbers listed in this book are area code 212 unless otherwise noted.

Subways are fast, and thus easier for children to ride than buses, so we provide subway directions, and bus routes only where essential. If you prefer to travel solely by bus, you can get all the information you need by calling 718-330-1234, a Transit Authority help line that is actually, of all things, helpful.

As of this writing, prices for the activities we recommend are moderate, by which we mean they are unlikely to cause more than the usual twitching as you reach for your wallet. When things get a little pricie—as in our Ten Treats (see page 113), for example—we tell you. But prices, as we all know too well, are subject to change; don't blame us if (when) they increase.

You are the best judge of whether your child is the proper age, gender, and type for the excursions we describe. So, with a few exceptions, we limit ourselves to telling you what there is to do and leave it to you to decide whether it's right for your family.

Chapter One

Into the Melting Pot:
Ethnic New York

A View of Old Manhattoes:
Inwood Hill Park with its *Indian caves* and *intense baseball players*, the *Dyckman Farmhouse Museum*, then lunch or a snack at *Carrot Top Pastries.*

At some point in their lives, Manhattanites—even the small ones—wonder what their island looked like before real estate developers started messing it up. The best surviving glimpse of that distant past is at Manhattan's northernmost tip, where **Inwood Hill Park** contains, among its nearly 200 acres, the largest natural woodlands on the island. Wear your climbing clothes for this one. Enter the park via Isham Park on Isham Avenue, passing the playing fields on your right; then bear to the right as the path diverges. Soon the foliage thickens, the walkway narrows and begins to climb, and the woods seem to loom: hickory, hackberry, yellow poplar, birch, sweetgum, spicebush (the twigs of which Native Americans used as chewing gum), and quaking aspen, whose leaves shimmer in the breeze.

Keep going until you see steep, rocky outcroppings up the hill on your left. The **caves** created by these overhanging ledges of rock were once inhabited by Indians. Time to leave the path; this climb is steep and requires some care, especially if the ground is wet. But it's not Everest, and in exchange for some huffing and puffing, you'll find deep, secluded niches in the rocks where the children can hunker down and you can remove yourself from the sights and sounds of the city. You may even see a shrew or vole—yes, this is true!—pleasantly rustic alternatives to New York's commoner rodents.

Once atop the cliffs, find the path that leads toward the Hudson River. The great view is even greater if you slip between the gaps in the chicken wire fencing on the path's river side.

When you come back down, pass the caves and go back down onto the original path. Continue along it until you come to a plaque where Peter Minuit's purchase of Manhattan Island from the Canarsie Indians was supposedly consummated. (In these leafy surroundings you can believe it, although those in the know say the deal was more likely closed at the Battery, where the Dutch had settled.)

Make sure to visit **The Nature Center**, operated by the Urban Park Rangers and housed in an old Columbia University boathouse. This friendly, busy place is action central for Park Ranger doings in northern Manhattan. Call ahead or get on the mailing list for advance word of its many activities. During the week, it's full of kids on school trips; weekends are devoted to lectures and hikes that families can do together. The rangers can point out fragments of wall scattered in the underbrush that mark where lavish homes (including that of Mr. Lord of Lord & Taylor) and a Revolutionary War–era fort once stood. They can show you where to gather nettles for soup or point out species of non-native trees, like copper beeches, that were planted by settlers and flourished. In season, there are canoe programs, planting and conservation projects, and a Winterfest. At least once a year, the Manhattan and Bronx rangers collaborate on the Manhattan to Bronx Connection, a guided hike around the park, over the Henry Hudson Bridge, and back.

At the top end of the park you'll see the turbulent Spuyten Duyvil, where the Hudson and Harlem rivers meet, not amicably. You're at the tip of Manhattan island. Rowers in skulls glide by from the Columbia boathouse. And, weather permitting, some of the most **exciting baseball** to be seen in New York (notwithstanding the Brooklyn Cyclones and the Staten Island Yankees) takes place on the diamonds up here. The teams are mostly Latin, and their game is skilled, hard-hitting, and ferociously competitive. And you're right up close to it. Stand behind the batting cage, watching fastballs whiz by and waiting for the crack of ball on bat. It's a lot more thrilling than a game on TV.

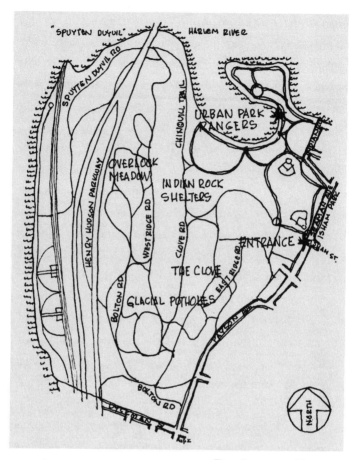

Afterwards, head downtown to the **Dyckman Farmhouse Museum** on Broadway, Manhattan's only surviving Dutch Colonial farmhouse. Built in 1784 and once the hub of a 450-acre spread, it has been painstakingly restored to its original condition and so it seems like a hallucination: a rustic antiquity on a completely urban street. Many of the objects on display belonged to the Dyckman family—though probably not the munitions, uniforms, and Hessian crockery you'll find in the Relic Room. The kitchen has great, sturdy cooking implements next to the open hearth. Right outside the kitchen window, scratched into the big stone outcropping, is a playing board for Nine Man Morris, an 18th-century children's game.

Two Hundred and Fourth Street is bustling, so food isn't hard to find. Diagonally across the street from the Dyckman Farmhouse is a Dunkin' Donuts. But a few blocks up Broadway is **Carrot Top Pastries**, owned by Renee Allen Mancino, whose renowned carrot cake has been called (in Molly O'Neill's *New York Cookbook*) the best in the world. This little pastry shop has a few tables and a small selection of sandwiches, quiches, and soups besides the home-baked goods (treat yourself to a hot apple pie as well). If you prefer, look for one of the many comfy Cuban-Chinese restaurants nearby, where children are welcome and can be made very happy with rice and beans, fried bananas, chicken and rice, and other not-too-spicy favorites. Remember, these Cuban-Chinese joints serve beer and wine, so pop a Corona and relax. The subway ride back home is always faster.

Inwood Hill Park (Isham Park entrance), Isham St. one block north of 207th St. and west of Broadway.)
The Nature Center, 304-2365.
Call to receive a copy of their calendar of events.
Dyckman Farmhouse Museum, 4881 Broadway at 204th St. 304-9422, http://www.dyckman.org/
Carrot Top Pastries, 5025 Broadway at 214th St. 569-1532
Getting there: Subway: A train to 207th St. or 1 to 215th St.

* *

Downtown, Back When:
Sights of the old Lower East Side,
including the **Lower East Side Tenement Museum, Eldridge Street Synagogue,**
and various venerable shops, then uptown to the East Village's hip emporia, ending with a casual meal at Telephone or Two Boots.

When the kids are old enough to be genuinely curious about the ways in which other people lived in other times, take a trip to the

Lower East Side, home to successive waves of immigrants from Ireland, Germany, Eastern Europe, the South, and Latin America. Despite the rising tide of hipness sweeping the nabe, echoes of that immigrant past are still to be seen here, nowhere more fully realized than at the **Lower East Side Tenement Museum** on Orchard Street.

This is a popular place; book your tickets before you show up, then pick 'em up at No. 90 Orchard. Get there early enough to watch the new video presentation produced for the museum by the History Channel. Then cross the street to No. 97, keeping in mind that the building has neither heat nor air-conditioning; in hot weather, fans and water are provided.

A guide leads you up the stoop and into a pitch-black hallway. The light (a 20th-century addition) comes on and you're standing in a deep, narrow space with dark custard-colored walls, doors opening off it, and a steep staircase to the apartments above. It's claustrophobic; it feels depressing and slumlike to 21st-century New Yorkers, but the guide gently reminds you that when this place was built in 1863, it was considered a desirable place to live. The tour takes in three apartments, painstakingly recreated to convey the lives of three families who lived there between the 1870s and the 1930s. With its dark, narrow hallways and cluttered little apartments, No. 97 fairly reeks of history.

For families, there's a wonderful special feature—a 45-minute visit to the Confino apartment, led by a guide costumed as 14-year-old Victoria Confino. The Confinos, Sephardic Jews, arrived from Turkey in 1916, and Victoria greets you as if you've just gotten off the boat, proudly showing you around the place and filling you in on what awaits you in New York. Kids will be astonished to talk to this charming, vivacious girl who doesn't know what television is, but is ecstatic to have a flush toilet instead of an outdoor privy. Victoria gets them to wind up the Victrola and handle such implements as the "washer agitator." If you're up for it, she'll teach you the foxtrot. And all along, she's talking about immigrant life on the Lower East Side—school, jobs, health, nickel movies at the nickelodeon, and who sleeps where when 10 people live in a one-bedroom apartment. It's riveting to hear all this "firsthand."

Everything about the museum is intelligently planned, from its website (where you can click on a little square of wallpaper to reveal the layer beneath, click again to find the next layer down, and so on) to the choice of volunteers, some of them old folks who grew up on the Lower East Side and delight in sharing their memories.

Afterwards, make a pit stop next door at **Il Laboratorio del Gelato** for ice cream that's handmade and intensely flavored, though not quite as intensely as the delicacies to be found just down the block at the new home of venerable **Guss Pickles**, the last word in Kosher pickles, made in the Bronx according to recipes known only to the owner. Full-sours are brined for 10 months; they are celestial, whatever the kids think.

Perked up by a sweet or sour snack, it's time to stroll, keeping in mind that on a Saturday, most of the Jewish businesses down here will be closed. At **Streit's Matzos**, the baking is done behind the counter, as it has been since 1925. Down Essex Street, peer into the window of **Rabbi M. Eizenbach's Religious Articles**, a dim, cluttered shop piled high with prayer shawls, books and philacteries, or **G&S Sporting Goods**, whose display does not look as if it's been changed since the '50s. Head over to 290 Henry Street to **St. Augustine's Episcopal Church**, which was built in the 1820s. If you call ahead, you may be able arrange to view the church's claustrophobic little gallery overlooking the nave, where slaves were permitted to worship. They were immigrants too, albeit reluctant ones (and they were traded downtown, at Pearl and Wall streets). Or you could head off to the long-neglected **Eldridge Street Synagogue**, built in the 1880s and once a sumptous place of stained glass and Depression-era marbleized wood paneling. Because it is now undergoing an elaborate restoration, visiting hours are limited, so call first.

If the kids are flagging by now, head uptown to **Katz's** on Houston, where rude old Jewish waiters serve enormous deli sandwiches. Just a knish's throw from Katz's is **Pomme-Pomme**, where Belgian fries come with a variety of sauces, including ketchup. Whichever you chose, stop in at **Economy Candy** afterward for chocolate band-aids, bubble gum cigars, and other candies that time forgot.

Head north to the East Village, your kitsch 'n' camp headquarters. **Love Saves the Day** has Davy Crockett hats and vintage lunchboxes; **Trash and Vaudeville** goes in for tiny tube skirts from England and magenta feather boas. Remember, stuff that looks this cheap seldom is; these places are pricey. Shrug it off, splurge, and gloat over your purchases at a casual East Village restaurant like **Telephone Bar & Grill**, which has a jolly red English phone box outside, and kid-pleasing bangers and mash or fish and chips inside. There's **Two Boots**, too, with its festive, tinselly decor, its combination Italian/Louisiana cooking (which actually works), and a patient and forgiving waitstaff that extends itself to make children feel at home. Sit down, cocktail in hand, and know that you've been good parents.

Lower East Side Tenement Museum, 90 Orchard St. cor. Orchard and Broome Sts. 431-0233, www.tenement.org/
Il Laboratorio del Gelato, 95 Orchard St. 343-9922
Guss Pickles, 85–87 Orchard St., Grand and Canal Sts. 254-4477
Eldridge Street Synagogue, 12 Eldridge St. just up from Division St. 219-0888, www.eldridgestreet.org

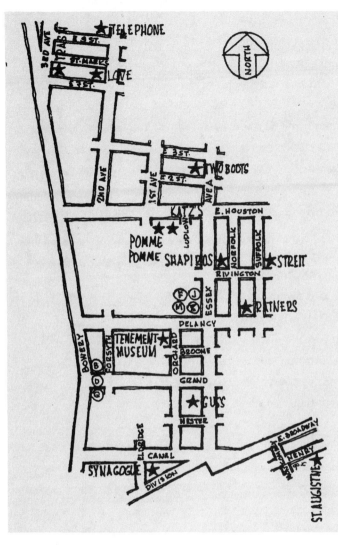

Streit's Matzos, 150 Rivington St. bet. Essex and Norfolk Sts. 475-7000, www.streitsmatzos.com

St. Augustine's Church, 290 Henry St., one block east of Chatham Sq., www.stangnyc.org

Katz's Delicatessen, 205 East Houston St., 254-2246, www.homedelivery.com/katz.html

Pomme-Pomme, 191 East Houston St., 646-602-8140

Economy Candy, 108 Rivington St., 254-1531,
www.economycandy.com

Love Saves the Day, 119 Second Ave. at 7th St. 228-3802

Trash & Vaudeville, 4 St. Marks Pl. bet. Second and Third Aves.
982-3590

Telephone Bar & Grill, 149 Second Ave. 529-5000,
www.telebar.com

Two Boots, 37 Avenue A bet. 2nd and 3rd Sts. 505-2276,
www.twoboots.com

Getting there: F train to Delancey St., J, M or Z train to Essex St.

* *

Near the Narrows:
In and Around *Bay Ridge*, from the
Nellie Bly Amusement Park
to Fort Hamilton's *Harbor Defense Museum*,
taking time out for *ice cream, parks*,
and, of course, the *Norwegian aspect*,
with bakeries, delis, and even a parade.

A community of prosperous farms and luxury second homes long
before it became a New York neighborhood, Bay Ridge has never
entirely merged with the city. It's been home to many successive
waves of immigrants (among the most recent arrivals are Syrians
and Greeks), and you'll find evidence of disparate cultures wherev-
er you look: Scandinavian bakeries, Italian delis, Irish pubs. Bay
Ridge also has the greatest density of restaurants anywhere in
New York—aside, of course, from Manhattan. But for kids, the
attractions are different; so different, in fact, that your first destination isn't even in Bay Ridge, but just west of it in Bensonhurst, or
Benson*hoist,* as the locals say.

Kids like amusement parks, but often their parents aren't
amused. Coney Island can be too rough, though it needn't be (see

page 86). The G-rated representatives of the genre, Great Adventure and Sesame Place, require hours of travel and pots of money. Fortunately, the discerning cool parent has an alternative: **Nellie Bly**, an amusement park you can be sure your small child will enjoy.

Nestled by the water, right off Shore Drive and just past Toys "R" Us, Nellie Bly is compact, a little shabby, and utterly benign. The rides are of the sweetly unthreatening variety—about the headiest are the bumper cars and the helter-skelter. Pretty much everything else is a variation on the carousel: planes in a circle, boats in a circle, motorcycles in a circle. The Fun House is nicely tame, although it does cough up the occasional weeping tot. Best of all, within an hour to 90 minutes, you'll have covered the whole thing, allowing you to return to a favorite ride or move on. The food is adequate and easy to find, as are the toilets. The result of all this? A good vibe, which you will see reflected in the people around you.

And what people! The families you'll see amount to a wonderful New York cross section. On a spring Sunday, you're likely to hear less English there than Yiddish, Russian, Chinese, Spanish, or Jamaican patois. Everybody's in a good mood, and there are many shared smiles of recognition as good-sport parents squeeze themselves onto tiny rides or cheer from the sidelines.

Afterwards, head for Fort Hamilton, a military base right at the foot of the Verrazano-Narrows Bridge that dates back to 1825. Here you'll find the small but fascinating **Harbor Defense Museum** housed in a little bunker called a *caponier* (French for "chicken coop"). It contains dioramas of naval battles, ship's models and antique weapons. Most impressive of all, it is on an actual military base; jeeps, cannons, and people in khaki are everywhere, guaranteed to keep children's heads swiveling. But beware: this museum's opening hours are highly variable and don't include weekends. So call first.

Next, head over to **Hinsch's** in Bay Ridge, a genuine old-fashioned coffee shop. It's bright and welcoming, and the waitresses are likely to call you "Sweetie." The clientele includes retirees, young moms with their babies, and famished ladies in recovery from shopping on bustling 86th Street. Hinsch's does all the classics well: tuna salad, open turkey sandwich, rice pudding. But it's the ice cream you're after. It's made on the premises and is, truly, something special. Many of the regulars are blue-haired Bay Ridge ladies munching egg salad sandwiches, cups of soup, and little dishes of butter pecan, so decorum is expected. But you can oblige—for the sake of the homemade ice cream, which is so good that conversation dwindles away when it's served. If it's pizza you're after, try **Lento's** on Third Avenue, where the crusts are so thin and crisp the locals call the pies Eucharist pizza.

From here, visit **Owl's Head Park** at the very northern edge of Bay Ridge. It's high, it has a new skate park, and New York Harbor is spread out before you. Just over the Belt Parkway, reachable via several footbridges, is **Shore Park**, the narrow ribbon of green that runs between the Parkway and the water. The sea breeze makes it a mecca for kiting enthusiasts. Fishermen, in-line skaters, and cyclists are out in force in all weather. And it was on one of these benches that John Travolta won Karen Lynn Gorney's heart, not to mention our own, in *Saturday Night Fever*. Don't even bother trying to explain it to Junior; you'll only embarrass yourself. If you've got the energy, you can walk a long way by the water, right under the Verrazano-Narrows Bridge (look up for a glimpse of peregrine falcons nesting) and as far as Bensonhurst Park.

P.S. Every May, on a Sunday between confirmation and Mother's Day, Bay Ridge holds its annual **Norway Independence Day Parade**, the high point of which is the crowning of Miss Norway herself. (You'd think they would crown her in Oslo, wouldn't you?) There are the requisite vintage cars, hand-pumping pols, and several bagpipe societies of hefty Hibernians (sometimes referred to as "cops in kilts"), and more willowy blonde teenagers than you could ever have imagined living in Brooklyn and owning ethnic Scandinavian outfits. (In fact, they come from three states.) At **Nordic Delicacies**, pick up some venison meatballs and lingonberry jam. Real Danish pastries and a loaf of sweet limpa bread from **Leske's Danish Bakery** should tide you over on the endless trip home via the R train, the local of locals.

Nellie Bly Amusement Park, 1824 Shore Pkwy. 718-996-4002
Harbor Defense Museum, Fort Hamilton, Fort Hamilton Pkwy. at 101st St. 718-630-4349
Hinsch's Confectionery, 8518 Fifth Ave. at 86th St., 718-748-2854
Lento's Restaurant, 7003 3rd Ave. nr. Ovington St. 718-745-9197
Owl's Head Park, Shore Rd. at 68th St. and Colonial Rd;
Shore Park, enter from Owl's Head Park, via 69th St. footbridge over the Belt Pkwy., or, if you're going down the Belt by car, stop and park at any of the parking places.
Norway Independence Day Parade, usually runs from 92nd St. up 5th Ave. to Leif Ericsson Park (at 67th St.); for details, call Evald Olson, 718-745-6653

Nordic Delicacies, 6909 3rd Ave. nr. 69th St. 718-748-1874
Leske's Danish Bakery, 7612 5th Ave. nr. 76th St. 718-680-2323
Getting there: Bay Ridge is best reached by car,
but if you have no choice, take the R train to 77th , 86th,
or 95th Sts. and bring some hefty amusements for the young.
For Nellie Bly, take Exit 5 off the Shore Parkway.

* *

Chinatown's Familiar Exotica:
Strolling, shopping, and eating, with stops at
a *museum*, a *Buddhist temple*, a *super-market* unlike any you've ever seen, *toy stalls* that sell critters, and an *arcade*. Whatever you do, don't forget *lunch* (as if!).

Here's a partial list of items you may buy on the bustling streets of Chinatown: tiny turtles, transformers, Kangol knockoffs, vases, slippers, shrines, live eels, miniature imitation stuffed animals, jade flowers, jade Buddhas, jade earrings, lots more jade, battery-operated hula girls and bathtub scuba divers, back scratchers, paper parasols, and dried shark fin for $185/lb. Is it any wonder that Chinatown is eternally exotic to children—and to their parents too?

Loud, bustling, and crowded, Chinatown is a tourist destination that is also still an immigrant world, with a proud history and an invigorating present. Unfamiliar smells, sights, and sounds are every-where, a wall-to-wall bazaar of weird merchandise and unfamiliar food. A walk through these twisty streets is always an adventure.

Start your visit with a painless history lesson at the

**Museum of Chinese
in the Americas**
on Mulberry Street. On the
second floor of a bustling
community center in a big

old schoolhouse, this small, kid-friendly museum conjures up, with objects, photographs, and documents, the hard world that Chinese immigrants faced when they came to America. Children will immediately notice the colorful dragon and the pagoda-shaped phone box; you can show them the eight-pound irons used by laundrymen and the tiny embroidered shoes made to fit bound feet.

Now for a look at what Chinatown has become: Stroll from Canal down Mulberry toward Chatham Square, the heart of Chinatown. Recently renovated Columbus Park on your right has a nice playground with a splash fountain that the little ones can cool off in. Check out the fish markets. Fish here is usually inexpensive and very fresh (sometimes still moving, in fact). Not of all of it looks familiar, either. On our last trip, we saw geoducks (giant clams), eels and mudfish, which we assure you looks a lot better than it sounds. Stalls brim with dried fish and meats and vegetables you may never have seen before. (Watch for a large melon with a spiky skin called a durian. If it's been cut open, you'll smell it before you see it!) Try the small mangos or some unknown dark green vegetable. Notice that the plastic bag is usually red (for good luck) and almost never white (for death). At the bottom of Mulberry, turn left and left again,then head up Mott, Chinatown's main artery.

It's good to know that nothing that happens to Chinatown, not even the tribulations endured by all the neighbors to Ground Zero, will ever diminish the precinct's sublime tackiness, and nowhere is this more fully realized than at the **_Chinatown Fair_** at 8 Mott Street, a dingy arcade with SuperPacman and other vintage games, as well as more current favorites. It's always busy and loud, full of local kids and tourists feeding quarters into their machines in an atmosphere of amiable grime and unsuitability. Your children will love it. Note the words in the center of the well-worn sign outside: "World Famo s [sic] Dancing & Tic-Tac-Toe . . ." Underneath there is a smudge, a ghost of the word that completed the sign: "Chickens." Gone but not forgotten.

Back on the street, it's tchotcke heaven. An immaculate shop called **Munchies Paradise** offers tiny candies in astonishing variety. Plenty of shops boast an impressive array of Digimon-, Pokemon-, and Dragonball Z-related comics, videos, and models. Keep an eye out for the big, elaborate transformer samurai sold at many newstands and by sidewalk vendors. Each is composed of smaller transformers; they tend to fall apart when handled, but they look great and the packaging has not one word of English on it, which impresses the children.

You can buy tiny turtles in Chinatown; you see them piled in little dishes of water in shops and on the street. Be warned: It's illegal to sell turtles under 4 inches in length and all of these are. But if you have the urge to invest in some adorable contraband, it'll cost you less than ten dollars. Of course, that doesn't include the hundred-or-so dollars worth of gear—tank, filter, light, heater—that you'll have to buy to insure that your turtle lives longer than a week. Still, the critters make excellent city pets: quiet, well-behaved, and smaller than a bichon frisé.

Meander down side streets. In shop windows on Doyers and Pell, you'll find mahjong and domino sets, decorative calendars, and wonderfully illustrated flash cards for learning English, each drawing accompanied by the appropriate Chinese and English words. (For a wider range of novelties, including Chinese checkers and lucky money envelopes, as well as books in English on martial arts and other subjects, try **Oriental Books and Stationery** at 29

East Broadway.) Step into one of the tiny herbalist shops that abound; your children's eyes will widen at the heaped ginseng roots, dried fungi, and ominous-looking potions and remedies on display.

There is a quieter aspect of Chinatown. Among the temples that dot the community, perhaps the most serene is the **Eastern States Buddhist Temple** at 64 Mott, with incense burning and bronze Buddhas gleaming in the candlelight. Senior citizens lounge in the anteroom, and there is a modest display of religious relics and statuary.

Finally, the moment of truth arrives; where are you going to eat? The celebrated **New York Noodletown**, on the Bowery, specializes in homemade guess-what in a no-frills but friendly atmosphere. Just south of Canal on Mott is the **Sweet 'n' Tart Cafe**, a small, tidy establishment whose menu, unusual even for Chinatown, includes gizzard, frog and, of all things, fresh fruit shakes, along with ever-popular dumplings, soups, and lo mein. Or be adventurous and pick your own lunch spot. Chinese food and children are a mutual admiration society; it's hard to go wrong down here. At the very worst, someone ends up eating a bun stuffed with crunchy duck feet.

Afterwards, stop in a local bakery like the **Golden Fung Wong** for an almond cookie or what look like enormous fried noodles dipped in honey, or go to **Saint's Alp Tea House** for a Pearl Tea—sweet, milky iced tea to which slightly chewy tapioca pearls have been added. The **Chinatown Ice Cream Factory** offers 36 homemade flavors including green tea and pineapple. This shop also sells a bright yellow T-shirt depicting a dragon eating a cone; it's a winner.

Finish up with a souvenir for yourself. At **Kam Man Food Products** on Canal, the pace is less hectic than on the

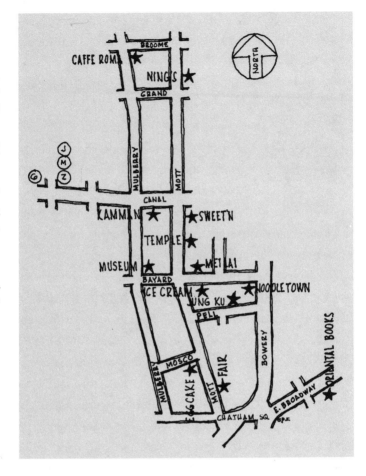

street, the range of merchandise is incredible, and the prices are low. Along with dozens of varieties of soy sauce, dried fish as big as your leg or small as your finger, Kam Man also sells cookware, cutlery, and serving dishes. Most important, it is one of the only places we have found that sells good-quality plastic sushi. These can easily become essential stocking stuffers.

If you've got any energy or appetite left, stroll up Mott to Little Italy, and stop in at the **Cafe Roma** for great cannoli and tortoni. Perched on spindly wrought-iron chairs, inspecting the day's purchases more closely, you'll all feel deeply cosmopolitan, which is only fitting.

Museum of Chinese in the Americas, Mulberry St. at Bayard St. 619-4785, http://www.moca-nyc.org/

Chinatown Fair, 8 Mott Street between Park Row and Pell St.

Oriental Books and Stationery, 29 E. Broadway between Catherine and Market St., 962-3634

Munchie's Paradise, 37 Mott St. 233-7650, www.ajichiban-usa.com

Eastern States Buddhist Temple of America, 64 Mott St. bet. Bayard and Canal Sts. 966-4753 (there is no English lettering on the sign, so look carefully)

New York Noodletown, 28 1/2 Bowery, 349-0923

Sweet 'n' Tart Cafe, 76 Mott Street, 334-8088 (A larger sister branch of Sweet'n'Tart has opened down the street at 20 Mott.)

Golden Fung Wong, 41 Mott Street, 267-4037

Saint's Alp Tea House, 51 Mott Street, 766-9889

Chinatown Ice Cream Factory, 65 Bayard Street, 608-4170

Kam Man Food Products, 200 Canal Street betweem Mulberry and Mott, 962-8414

Cafe Roma Pastry, 385 Broome St. cor. Mulberry St. 226-8413

Getting there: 6, J, M, N, Q, R, Z to Canal St.

Chapter Two

Museums: New Ways
to Look at Old Things

Brooklyn's Best:
From the *Brooklyn Museum of Art* to the
Botanic Garden and *Grand Army Plaza*,
with time out at the *Greenmarket*
and *the heavenly luncheonette*
that time forgot.

If the **Brooklyn Museum of Art** were somewhere
else, it would be a premier attraction for tourists and local culture
vultures alike. It has world-class collections (especially Egyptian,
African, and Native American) and a building that looks the way a
world-class museum is supposed to look—grand and looming. (And
soon, it will also have a striking new glass and steel entrance.) It has
its own subway stop and a parking lot of respectable size. And it's
next door to the superb Brooklyn Botanic Garden. Even with all this
going for it, the museum is rarely crowded—except on the first
Saturday night of each month, when admission is free and there are
special events. On a weekend afternoon, it's a great place to visit.

Start on the fifth floor in the American Identities exhibit. It's very
kid-friendly, the art augmented by videos and posted comments by
children about specific works. The beautiful pastoral landscapes by
Thomas Cole and William Sidney Mount are full of fascinating
details. August Aaron Wilson's big carved tigers, done in a primitive
style, look like giant toys that more than one child will want to take
home. One floor down, the furnished period rooms allow kids to
peer into the past. Search out the Victorian parlor with a long dou-
ble line of small wooden animals winding across the floor to a
Noah's Ark. The stained glass panels near the elevators are all
exquisite, but the memorial panel by Walter Cole Brigham is the
most enchanting, made of chunks of glass as thick as jewels.

Next, the mummy in the Egyptian collection; it's real! There's
also a wonderful gold ibis which has become the Museum's un-
official mascot. Then back down to the ground floor with its

towering totem poles, spooky masks, and New World artifacts. There's a well-stocked gift shop here and a learning center where, on weekends, four to seven-year-olds and their parents can join Arty Facts, a drop-in art program (call for times).

The light-filled, pretty Museum Cafe is on the first floor; it has salads, sandwiches, and burgers made to order. You can also walk through the parking lot to the **Brooklyn Botanic Garden**, where there's good chili, sandwiches, and ice cream to be had while basking among the Conservatory greenhouses (better yet, save your appetite for Tom's Restaurant—see below). Each of the four greenhouses is a different little world with its own climate: In the rain forest, the kids will get a kick out of the perpetual drips and the towering banana tree with its drooping load of fruit; in the desert, the motley array of cacti is stunning.

The newly restored Japanese Garden is serene and beautiful. That brilliant vermillion, gatelike structure gracing the pond is called a torii, and it indicates the presence of a shrine, which you'll find in the pine grove just beyond the torii. There are turtles, ducks, and giant carp to feed (the ducks prefer whole wheat bread). Stroll the little path around the pond. If you're lucky, a heron or egret will glide overhead to its nest in a neighboring tree.

When its thousands of species are blooming, the Rose Garden can make even the youngest jaw drop. Call for information about the Cherry Blossom Festival, which offers not just acres of blooms, but also Japanese music, dancing, and impressive martial arts demonstrations.

If it's Saturday, stroll down to **Grand Army Plaza**, and check out the **Greenmarket** for Ronnybrook chocolate milk, real Amish people, and the dour sheep farmers who, in addition to their lamb products, often bring wool and a working spinning wheel. Each spring and fall, the majestic **Soldiers and Sailors Arch** is open for a gallery show, Art in the Arch. Climb the hundred or so steps to take in new art and a spectacular view of Prospect Park, the harbor, and the city; or linger at ground level to watch newlyweds stepping out of white limos to be photographed in front of the fountains.

If you have time and appetites on your hands, head straight across Eastern Parkway and down Washington Avenue to **Tom's Restaurant**, an old-fashioned luncheonette festooned with artificial flowers and signs touting the cherry lime rickeys, egg creams, and banana-walnut pancakes. Everyone's friendly (especially owner Gus Vlahadas, who has been called "the friendliest man in Brooklyn"); the burgers are managable for small hands, the fries are crisp, and the egg salad not too mayonnaisey. It's not only the children who'll feel welcome.

Brooklyn Museum of Art, 200 Eastern Pkwy. at Washington Ave. 718-638-5000, www.brooklynart.org/
Brooklyn Botanic Garden, 1000 Washington Ave. 718-622-4433, www.bbg.org/
Greenmarket at **Grand Army Plaza**, Flatbush Ave. at Eastern Parkway
Soldiers and Sailors Arch at **Grand Army Plaza** 718-287-3400
Tom's Restaurant, 782 Washington Ave. at Sterling Pl. 718-636-9738
Getting there: On a sunny Saturday, take the 2 or 3 train to Eastern Pkwy (East Siders, take the 4 or 5 train to Nevins St.,then walk across the platform). Get out at the Brooklyn Museum stop and you're there.

Queens of Arts (and Sciences):
An easy subway trip into *Flushing Meadows, Queens,* to see the *Unisphere*, the *Panorama of the City of New York*, the *Hall of Science*, and other delights. Finally, epiphanies for all at *Pearson's Barbecue.*

Flushing Meadows in Queens has many delights, and you can explore them without the hassle of a car. It's positively liberating to find yourself in such a wide and grassy space after stepping off the subway. There are enough things to do for a couple of trips. If you're heading here for the first time, you've got choices to make.

This is, of course, the place where two celebrated World's Fairs were held. Checking on their remains has the thrill of an archaeological dig for adults, while the scale of the surviving structures alone will make the kids giddy and exultant. You won't be able to stop them from racing toward the gigantic *Unisphere*—which you've undoubtedly seen many times from the accursed LIE (isn't it nice to be looking the other way?)—so follow along and prepare to be amazed. You are looking at the largest globe in the world. Made for the '64 fair, the spherical grid with steel plates for continents is 140 feet high and weighs 700,000 pounds. In the summer, fountains play around it. Prepare for much frolicking on the steps around the pool; bring skateboards (it's a great, safe space), and the camera.

Next door, the *Queens Museum of Art*, home to the Panorama of the City of New York, an architectural scale model of the whole city. At last count, it contained 895,000 tiny buildings as well as highways, bridges, and other landmarks. You can walk around the edge of the whole area on a glass-bottomed ramp built a few feet above it. The room is subdued, with rapt people pointing and peering, trying to find where they live. At regular intervals, a little plane takes off from La Guardia, the sky darkens, and little lights gleam from within the houses as night falls. It's a heady experience, especially for kids; for once, they're bigger than all of New York City. Don't forget to bring binoculars, which make it much easier to search for your building.

Across Grand Central Parkway, within easy walking distance over a little bridge, is the **New York Hall of Science**, another wondrous '64 relic built in the shape of an undulating curtain. It's a welcome antidote to those burned out by the Liberty Science Center; there's no glitz to bombard you, no big crowds to distract. Instead, there's a low-key and peaceful hands-on museum which gives children umpteen scientific tricks to do. If they're old enough, they can learn from them; if they're really young, they'll just have a great time playing. There are giant bubbles and a 400-pound pendulum whose swing you can alter with magnets. You can make music on big pan pipes that pick up the ambient sound of the room, create optical illusions, mix colors, observe bacteria through a microscope, and power a fan as you pedal a bike. There's as much opportunity to move as there is to sit, and the friendly young staff is well able to pull a shy youngster into the swim. At the groovy new science playground outside, you can climb a steel-reinforced rope web, experiment with leverage on a giant seesaw, bounce your voice, and make water climb and cascade. The playground is only for kids six and up, and there's a nominal extra charge to get in. The excellent gift shop features an inexpensive "starter" microscope; the inevitable astronaut ice cream is (and kids will concur) disgusting enough to put you right off space travel. The vending machine food in the cafeteria isn't much better, so hold out.

The compact **Queens Wildlife Center** is next door and most appealing. It's got impressive South American spectacled bears; immense bison and elk; and a geodesic-domed aviary in which hawks, turkeys, and gaudy, green monk parakeets, among other species, soar, strut, and perch. The sweet petting zoo has the usual farmyard atmosphere and animals (but also llamas!). Nearby is the Playground for All Children, whose equipment and layout have been sensitively designed to accommodate kids with special physical needs.

By now, someone's probably ready to eat. Fortunately, you're only two blocks from the **Lemon Ice King of Corona**, a chrome-clad classic that always has twenty-odd (some very odd) flavors on hand, including peanut butter and chocolate. Nothing's better on a hot day.

But there's a challenge here, and it's saving room for another of Queens's culinary delights, just a few stops away on the 7 train: **Pearson's Barbecue** (formerly Stick to Your Ribs), simply the best 'cue in New York. The atmosphere is decidedly casual. Located in the back of Legends Sports Bar, Pearson's consists of a handful of wooden tables where you can chomp blissfully on fragrant trays of meat brought from the wood-burning pit outside while staring absently at sports on TV. You dine off paper plates, and the food—brisket, ribs, chicken, chopped pork on sweet Portuguese rolls, outstanding fries and beans, coleslaw, cobblers, and brownies— is sublime.

Queens Museum of Art, Flushing Meadows Corona Park, Queens 718-592-9700, http://www.queensmuse.org/
New York Hall of Science, Flushing Meadows Corona Park, Queens 718-699-0005, http://www.nyhallsci.org/
Queens Wildlife Center, Flushing Meadows Corona Park, Queens 718-271-1500, http://wcs.org/home/zoos/queenswildlife-center

Note: On summer weekends, a trolley bus runs between Flushing Meadows's various attractions; a single fare lets you use it all day.

Lemon Ice King of Corona, 52-02 108th Street, 718-699-5133

Pearson's Texas Barbecue/Legends, 71-04 35th Ave., Jackson Heights 718-779-7715

Getting there: To get to Flushing Meadows, take the No. 7 train from Times Square to Willets Point/Shea Stadium. To get to Pearson's, take the 7 back toward Manhattan to 74th St. and Broadway or the E, F, G or R to Broadway and Roosevelt (it's the same stop).

* *

Naval Engagement:
A day at the ***Intrepid Sea Air Space Museum***, topped off with a meal at a zingy ***fifties diner*** or the ***Cupcake Cafe.***

A trip to the ***Intrepid***, way west on 46th Street, makes for a full-size afternoon. The museum encompasses several ships clustered around a visitors' center and can look a little daunting, but resist the temptation to try the adjacent Circle Line Tour instead, unless your kid is up for three hours on a boat listening to somebody talk. This museum is a thrilling outing.

The retired naval craft here range in size from an old harbor

tug to the Intrepid itself, an immense aircraft carrier which served in the Second World War and Vietnam and was also for a time NASA's "prime recovery vessel." Begin your tour on the Intrepid's hangar deck. Ancient planes and battered space capsules dangle from the ceiling; the kids will make a beeline for the genuine fighter-plane cockpit (it's hard to imagine how anyone larger than a child could sit in it, actually). Much of the space is given over to the Intrepid's role in World War II, with elaborate table models of some of the ship's major engagements. The models have the appeal of toys but are necessarily glass-encased to protect them from little fingers. Still, your kids will be thrilled by the details—a Japanese airplane smaller than your pinkie attempts to escape the great ship, but it trails a wispy cloud of cotton smoke, indicating it's been hit. Nearby, full-size military equipment includes a bathosphere, which jockeys for attention with the "thrill simulator," a ride that rotates passengers upside down and sideways simultaneously. This may be how astronauts train, but not right after lunch. On the hangar deck, you can get a dog tag stamped with your name while you wait. They start at under $10 depending on the metal (go for the plain Armed Forces Issue), and they're irresistible.

Before you move on, find the plaque marking the spot where a kamikaze plane hit the ship during World War II, killing thirty-odd crewmen. When you get to the words "You are standing on hallowed ground," the gravity of the place will touch you.

Clamber up onto the bridge, where weather-beaten, retired sailors are glad to explain what all the buttons and switches do. Then wander below decks, where you'll find atmospheric tableaux of life-size mannequins. These are done with a real sense of theater. In one cramped room, a group of officers plot coordinates for the guns. Details like half-filled coffee cups, overflowing ash trays, and moody lighting heighten the drama (and might frighten the smallest kids). The descriptions accompanying these exhibits are fun to read and informative, especially the one that explains the U_2 spy-plane scandal and another that explains how heli-copters take off and land vertically.

On the wide, breezy flight deck you'll see an array of planes and heli-copters. These are the real thing, so if your children should remark that the lethal-looking Bluebird reminds them of Star Wars, point out that it is in fact the fastest plane in the world.

Before leaving the carrier, walk to the end of the deck and look north. You can see the Little Red Lighthouse (a rare shore view) nestled under the New York pier of the George Washington Bridge (see p. 59). If it's a weekend between April and October, you might find yourself smiling at pleasure-seekers in life jackets, gamely practicing a lifeboat drill as their cruise ship prepares to embark from the passenger ship terminals next door.

If you're over six and/or can still fit through the small hatchway at its entrance, join the line to enter the Growler, the only guided-missile submarine in the world that's open to the public. This claustrophobic vessel can only accommodate 17 reasonably lean and limber visitors at a time.

The visitors' center contains a theater and the gift shop (but nothing beats the dog-tags). The mess hall serves near-authentic navy chow, and there a fast food joint for the fainter of heart. But we recommend heading east toward Ninth Avenue, one of the city's great food bazaars. On the way, you could stop at the huge and gaudy **Market Diner** on Eleventh Avenue and 43rd, with everything on the menu from lobster tails to waffles. On Ninth, the cute and funky **Cupcake Cafe** is famous for its you-know-whats, and also for its muffins, donuts, and cookies. For older kids, try early dinner at one of the dear old French restaurants (**Chez Napoleon** or **Tout va Bien**) dating back to the days of the ocean liners. Go early, before the pre-theater rush and see if anyone's up for escargots.

Intrepid Sea Air Space Museum, W. 46th St. and 12th Ave.
245-0072, http://www.intrepidmuseum.org/

Market Diner, 572 Eleventh Ave. at 43rd St., 695-0415

Cupcake Cafe, 522 Ninth Ave. at 39th St. 465-1530

Chez Napoleon, 365 W. 50th St. bet. Eighth and Ninth Aves.
265-6980

Tout va Bien, 311 W. 51st. St. bet. Eighth and Ninth Aves.
265-0190

Getting there: From the nearest subway stop at 42nd Street
and Eighth Avenue, you still have to walk four blocks north
and four long blocks west. The M 50 bus stops right at the Intrepid,
however.

* *

Guggenheim vs. Whitney.
Into every young life some modern art must fall: But where do you start?

These grand Upper East Side institutions offer fine collections of
modern art in small dosages, well suited for the young. Each trip
makes an interesting outing, with room for something else. But
which will be more rewarding? That is the question. And here are
the answers:

Location, Location, Location

The Whitney's closer to the subway, but the Guggenheim's
closer to the park and to another short-and-sweet museum. The
Museum of the City of New York is still only a few blocks away and
has some extraordinary dollhouses and antique toys.

Certainly, the Whitney's pretty close to the park, too, but its
nearest neighbors, museum-wise, are the Met (too much for this
trip) and the Frick (under 16 not allowed).

Advantage: Guggenheim.

The Venue

While some question the Guggenheim's merits as an exhibition space, no one can deny that it's a great playground. For a start, more than one child has been known to compare the main tower to a gigantic toilet bowl; the giggles begin at that point. Inside, the space inspires action. Children race up and down the sloped floors and shout across the cavernous spiral. Be prepared for the art to be upstaged by stairway landings good for hiding. If you want your kids to look properly at the exhibits, don't start at the top of the ramp, which presents them with an irresistible downward slope. Instead, conduct your tour in a stately way, uphill.

The Whitney, on the other hand, is an interesting building if you like that sort of thing, but no one will ever mistake it for a toilet bowl. The single ticket booth and the solitary elevator (albeit a large one) create minor annoyances.

Advantage: Guggenheim again.

The Staff

The Guggenheim often teems with throngs of kids, and inevitably some of them run, shout, and, of course, try to touch the art, especially if the art is a big, soft, fabric slice of pie, which it might be. Perhaps that's why guards and clerks at the Guggenheim project a quality of having seen everything a museum guard can possibly see; nothing fazes them. As long as you don't touch the art, they are pleasant and helpful.

Whitney guards are cool and a little pushy, always realigning the omnipresent ticket queue. It must come from working on Madison Avenue.

Yet again, Guggenheim gets the nod.

The Food

The Guggenheim's cafeteria is small, but pleasantly decorated with the sort of swooping lines and curvy chairs you see on "The Jetsons." They serve modest cafeteria food at a modest museum markup.

The Whitney's food service consists of a sit-down cafe and a little snack stand with pricey sandwiches, coffees, snacks, and a few seats at a counter. There's usually a wait for the cafe.

Ho-hum. Where'd you rather eat?

Guggenheim again.

The Gift Shops

Both offer standard museum merchandise: lovely art books, prints, cards, ties, etc. and tasteful toys that won't get as much use as the prices demand.

Draw.

The Art

By far the most important exhibit at the Guggenheim is Frank Lloyd Wright's. Beyond that, the Chagalls make an impact; they remind kids of dreams and fairy tales.

The Whitney's permanent collection (on the 5th floor) includes Alexander Calder's *Circus*, which thrills children, and a very realistic sculpture of a leg sticking out of a wall with a candle growing out of its knee. Don't miss Charles Simonds's *Dwellings*, which looks like a miniature Pueblo village and sits on a ledge off the landing between the second and third floors, or Dennis Oppenheim's *Lecture #1*, a doll-size figure delivering an endless, soporific talk to row upon row of miniature chairs. There are major works by such favorites as Hopper, O'Keeffe, and Warhol, but be warned: some of the works here are probably too graphic for children under 10 or so. On the other hand, the Gaston Lachaise nude that greets you as you come off the 5th-floor elevator does tend to induce giggles.

Advantage: Ours is not to evaluate the art of these museums, only to suggest that the Whitney makes it easy for a young person to focus on the art, so the Whitney wins this one.

Final Score: Guggenheim: 5, Whitney: 2.

Conclusion: Of course you'll go to both, but why not start with the Guggenheim? And if it goes horribly wrong, you're closer to the park than the toy stores.

The Solomon R. Guggenheim Museum, 1071 Fifth Ave. at 88th St. 423-3500, www.guggenheim.org
Museum of the City of New York, Fifth Ave. at 103rd St. 534-1672, www.mcny.org
The Whitney Museum of American Art, 945 Madison Ave. at 75th St. 570-3676, www.whitney.org
Getting there: For the Guggenheim, the 4, 5, or 6 train to 86th St.; for the Whitney, the 6 train to 77th St.

* *

SoHo Art Trek:

An intriguing and accessible tour featuring the New York Earth Room and The New Museum of Contemporary Art, as well as nifty buildings, shopping, and food with transgenerational appeal.

There's more to SoHo than chic shopping and crowds. Start at the **New York Earth Room** on Wooster Street. The entrance is poorly labeled, and the stairs are rickety. But once you get to the top you're face-to-face with a permanent installation of crumbly brown earth—280,000 pounds of it—piled to a level height of about 22 inches, spread across a white-walled loft space, and separated from you only by a Plexiglas partition that can be reached over. Not much going on here, only the occasional mushroom or weed poking its way up. What's so marvelous is simply the presence of the vast, brown living expanse; it almost seems to breathe. Some people become so attached to it that they come back again and again, and breathe along with it. (Note: the Earth Room is closed from June to September.)

Now head across Prince Street to Broadway (with maybe a stop at **Untitled** for postcards of every kind), and head north to a museum that is perfect for kids: **The New Museum of Contemporary Art**. The space is large and loftlike. It holds eclectic and eye-catching work—neon, video, performance art, sculptures made of everything from beads to branches and silky-smooth marble.

Art creates a hearty appetite, which in this neighborhood can present a problem. People with older kids could head for **Spring Street Natural**, which offers varied, accessible vegetarian food in a cheerful setting or, in the other direction, the low-key **Cupping Room Cafe**, at West Broadway and Broome, for good pasta or hamburgers (the kitchen will produce small portions on request). Another good choice is the **New Era Café** on Broadway, a breezy, high-ceilinged place with salads, pastas, and enough room between tables to accommodate strollers. If your children are in an unreceptive mode, consider the Sabrett's man who is usually to be found on the street just south of the Guggenheim. A hot dog eaten in the open air is one of New York's supreme delights, after all. If it's raining, or you need to sit down, there is a pizza parlor on Broadway: **Piccola Pizza**.

After lunch, those with young children should drop in at the **Children's Museum of the Arts**, a friendly, messy beehive of artistic activity. No looking here, just participation. Then on to the **New York City Fire Museum**, with its impressive displays of vintage equipment, a taxidermied dog from the '30s with a heroic fire-fighting history, and a very loud bell kids can ring. The excellent gift shop has rubber Dalmatians and fireman transformers, among other treats. Back on Broadway, the new **Scholastic Store** is full of Harry Potteriana and more, but don't miss **The Enchanted Forest** on Mercer Street, a quirky little toy shop decked out as a forest. It's not cheap, but the soft toys, wooden flutes, and puppets are lovely.

With older children, you can keep walking through SoHo, either crisscrossing your way downtown between Broadway and West Broadway or choosing the streets that are your favorites for **cast-iron architecture**—Greene Street has the most and the best-preserved. Broadway has three real beauties: the Singer Building (1904) at 561–563, the St. Nicholas Hotel at 521–523 (it was used as a Union Army headquarters during the Civil War—look up to see it at its best), and the Haughwout Building at 488–492 (the first building to use a steam safety elevator).

A choice of final stops—**Canal Jean** on Broadway, for the hip and fashion-conscious (great prices, wide and wild selection), or **Pearl Paint** on Canal Street, for your artsy kid. This is the preeminent craft store in the city, and it's not just aimed at children; so it's as well to know what you're looking for before you attack the five floors of beeswax, plaster of Paris, whittling tools, model kits, colored sand, and papier-mâché. When you come out of either store, laden with thrilling purchases, Chinatown (see page 28) will be beckoning. But you should save it for another day.

New York Earth Room, 141 Wooster St. 989-5566, www.diacenter.org/ltproj/er/

Untitled, 159 Prince St. bet. W. Broadway and Thompson St. 982-2088

The New Museum of Contemporary Art, 583 Broadway bet. Prince and Houston Sts. 219-1222, www.newmuseum.org/

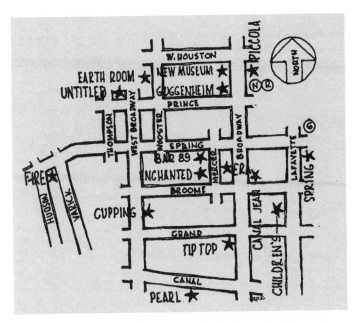

Spring Street Natural, 62 Spring St. at Lafayette St. 966-0290

Cupping Room Cafe, 359 W. Broadway bet. Broome and Grand Sts. 925-2898

New Era Café, 495 Broadway bet. Spring and Broom 274-0891

Piccola Pizza, 594 Broadway bet. Prince and Houston 274-1818

The Children's Museum of the Arts, 182 Lafayette St. bet. Broome and Grand Sts., 274-0986 or 941-9198, www.cmany.org

New York City Fire Museum, 278 Spring St. bet. Hudson and Varick Sts., 691-1303, www.nycfiremuseum.org

Scholastic Store, 557 Broadway bet. Prince and Spring Sts., 343-6166

The Enchanted Forest, 85 Mercer St. between Spring and Broome, 925-6677

Canal Jean Co., Inc., 504 Broadway bet. Spring and Broome Sts. 226-0737 or 226-1130 for tape

Pearl Paint Co. Inc., 308 Canal St. bet. Broadway and Church St. 431-7932

Getting there: Take the N or R train to Prince St; C, E, or 6 train to Spring St.

* *

The *Metropolitan Museum of Art* x 2: A first foray and a second trip for your budding connoisseurs.

Nothing ventured, nothing gained.

For that first trip to the Met, stage a quick guerilla action, and then escape before the sheer size of the place becomes oppressive. Begin with **Ancient Egypt**: it never fails to enthrall and it's right there, on the ground floor, past the huge recumbent lion. The massive sarcophagi are jaw-dropping, while the 23 Mekutra models (tiny industrious clay people found in a tomb, busily at work carting grain, rowing, weaving) will bring delighted smiles. William, the Met's blue hippo mascot, is somewhere around; ask a guard for directions. Kids' eyes widen at the sight of the Temple of Dendur, especially when you show them the photos of it in situ so that they can grasp the engineering feat that brought it to New York.

Now, a kid-friendly design coup. Behind the Temple, through a glass door, there's a selection from the Burdick Collection of **baseball trading cards**! These delights will sustain you as you head for the **armor**. Highlights here include the medieval knights on horseback, a child's suit of armor, and the ferocious samurai warrior in a suit made of steel and leather scales, laced together with leather and silk. Awesome, for once, is the appropriate word. Finally, in complete contrast, spend some time in the soothing space of **Engelhard Court**, an indoor sculpture garden that features a Louis Comfort Tiffany fountain.

P.S. The Met does a wonderful book for children called *Inside the Museum* by Joy Richardson (published by the Metropolitan Museum of Art/Harry N. Abrams). Try to get a copy before you go, and the kids will be primed.

Second try

Capitalize on your previous success, and venture upstairs, where you'll find Emanuel Gottlieb Leutze's **Washington Crossing the Delaware**. It is the largest painting in the museum, and the perfect place to start, because of its heroic scale and subject, and also because it contains three glaring historical inaccuracies. If you've read about the painting beforehand in *Inside the Museum*, the kids will have fun finding the mistakes; and while you're at it, compare **George Washington** portraits (Gilbert Stuart's is here). Take in the Edward Hoppers and George Caleb Bingham's *Fur Traders* Descending the Missouri en route to the period rooms (building up to a Frank Lloyd Wright living room from a Minnesota house, a low-ceilinged, modernist beauty). Next, walk selectively through the European paintings. Rubens's voluptuous nudes will embarrass most kids, but the perfect details of rustic life in **Bruegel's The Harvesters** or the dotty splendor of the Seurats fascinate. All the big names are here— Rembrandt, Van Gogh, Raphael— but head for surer territory, namely, the **Department of Modern Art**, which teems with big, bold, witty paintings and structures that grab the attention of young visitors. Next time, they'll have their own favorites to visit.

The Metropolitan Museum of Art, 1000 Fifth Ave. bet. 80th and 84th Sts. 535-7710, www.metmuseum.org
Getting there: the 4,5 or 6 train to 86th St. and Lexington Ave.

Chapter Three
The City's Best-kept Secrets
(right under your nose)

Brooklyn Down Under:

A visit to *the world's oldest subway tunnel* and the *Transit Museum*, a dawdling stop over *ice cream* and *Middle Eastern treats*, and, finally, the city's second-best view, from *the Promenade in the Heights.*

Brooklyn's oldest **subway tunnel** is also the world's oldest, and it's the singular passion of its (re)discoverer, Brooklyn native and railroad buff **Robert Diamond**, who conducts tours of his find when he feels like it. Make one of these tours the centerpiece of a day in, around, and under Brooklyn Heights.

Legends of Brooklyn's lost rail tunnel have existed for years. Robert Diamond heard them and set about finding the tunnel. After months of poring over ancient documents and newspapers and annoying city officials with his investigations, Diamond got permission to poke around underground. He went down a manhole at the intersection of Atlantic and Court, broke through a wall, and a 150-year-old breeze blew into his face.

That was in 1979. Since then, Mr. Diamond and a hard core of volunteers, the Brooklyn Historic Railway Association, have been slowly excavating the site. About a quarter mile of tunnel has been cleared. Mr. Diamond intends to keep digging right to the waterfront in Red Hook, where the track begins. He has more plans too, which he will enthusiastically share with you when he's not explaining tunnel-boring technology of the 1840s; why the developer who built the tunnel had it sealed not 25 years later; and why it was reopened in 1916, wired for electricity, then promptly shut.

Diamond's a spellbinding raconteur, and he has a few blood-

curdling anecdotes that will delight the children. (One unpopular foreman, for instance, was murdered and mixed into the mortar, so he is still, literally, on-site.) The entrance to the tunnel, down that manhole in the middle of Court and Atlantic, is a squeeze, and folks with claustrophobic leanings will feel a frisson. But the brick-lined tunnel itself, with its impressively high, arched ceiling, is stately and calming. The silence is total, with no hint of the traffic thundering above. Bring a flashlight and comfy shoes, and keep your eyes peeled for crickets, old nails and hardware, and 19th-century graffiti.

The New York City Transit Museum,

housed in a decommissioned subway station two blocks away, is due to reopen in 2003 after renovation. The exhibits of gears and turnstiles will intrigue the children, while the tokens, ads, maps, and Miss Subway tchotchkes will carry Proustian echoes for parents. Most evocative are the vintage subway cars that you can get into. Students of subway strap design will note a clear deterioration over the years. The renovation promises to bring enhanced video programs.

Now back to Atlantic Avenue, for a restorative food stop. There are various possibilities: **Atlantic Bagel** for bagels and sandwiches; **Brawta**, a two-block walk down Atlantic and a bright, bustling, and wildly successful Caribbean restaurant (where you can easily find a non-spicy item for the kids); or **Ben and Jerry's** which, with its post-hippie décor and formidable array of flavors and toppings, is always bustling with gleeful, smudge-faced kids and parents who seem to have temporarily abandoned their diets and said yes to temptation. To them we say: Wise move.

Before leaving Atlantic Avenue, stop in at **Sahadi**, the Middle Eastern Zabar's (closed on Sundays), for Swiss chocolate bars, loose spices, fresh halvah, olives, dried fruit, pistachios by the bushel, and great hummus and keftah for supper at home—aaah! The aromas are great, and so are the prices. No credit cards, though. And of course you can't leave without investing in some flaky, sticky Middle Eastern pastries and cookies—stock up on them and on spinach pies at the **Damascus Bread & Pastry Shop**, a few doors down from Sahadi.

If you have the energy, just a few blocks away there's one great sight that's not to be missed. Walk through the leafy, narrow streets of the Heights to the **Promenade**: take in the extraordinary and newly poignant view of Manhattan. If the Promenade looks familiar even though you've never been there before, it's because every advertising spread in New York City seems to be shot there.

P.S. You can give any real train aficionados in your home a glimpse of the ornate and unused **City Hall subway station**, which is rented out to television and film producers. Take the East Side downtown local to the last stop. Remain in the last car while it turns around for the uptown journey. Grab a glimpse of the station out the back window as the train pivots by.

Subway Tunnel, visit the Historic Brooklyn Railroad Association website to find out when Robert Diamond is leading his tunnel tour. www.brooklynrail.org

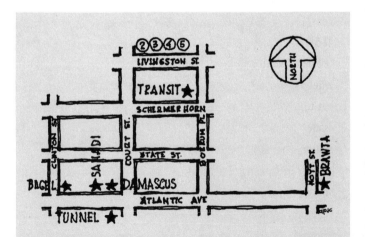

New York City Transit Museum, Schermerhorn St. and Boerum Pl. 718-243-3060 www.mta.nyc.ny.us/museum/index.html

Atlantic Bagel, 177 Atlantic Ave. bet. Clinton and Court Sts. 718-330-0303

Brawta, 347 Atlantic Ave. at Hoyt St. 718-855-5515

Ben and Jerry's, 156 Court St. between Pacific and Amity Sts.

Sahadi Importing Co. Inc., 187 Atlantic Ave. bet. Clinton and Court Sts. 718-624-4550

Damascus Bread & Pastry Shop Ltd., 195 Atlantic Ave. bet. Clinton and Court Sts. 718-625-7070

Promenade, East River shore bet. Montague and Orange Sts.

Getting there: 2, 3, 4, or 5 train to Borough Hall.

The tunnel tours begin outside the Independence Savings Bank on the southwest corner of Court St. and Atlantic Ave.

* *

In the shadow of the Great Gray Bridge:
Fort Washington Park and the Little Red Lighthouse, and, since you're up here, how could you miss a chance to visit The Cloisters?

Unless you live in the neighborhood, just getting to **Fort Washington Park** is a challenge. But it's worth it. This little-known strip of green runs along the west shore of Manhattan, parallel to Washington Heights and right next to the water, 155th Street to Dyckman Street; it offers great views of the river and the Palisades, woodsy trails, loads of facilities—baseball diamonds, basketball and tennis courts, a playground—and an ambience that's dreamy and tucked-away. During spring and summer the baseball diamonds are always in use, mostly by Little League teams, but (take note, tennis players) the courts are seldom fully occupied.

And of course it's got the **Little Red Lighthouse**. Since it's not easily seen from our shores (or even the George

Washington Bridge), the lighthouse has assumed mythic status, something everybody's heard of but no one's visited. However, it is undeniably there, tiny and red and nestled sweetly at water's edge right under the GWB. And just as it is in Hildegarde Hoyt Swift's classic story, *The Little Red Lighthouse and the Great Gray Bridge*, the diminutive building is full of personality:

It was round and fat and red.

It was fat and red and jolly.

And it was VERY, VERY PROUD.

The 75-year-old lighthouse sits on rocks where there once stood a gibbet used to execute pirates. During spring and summer, it's occasionally open for the Urban Park Rangers' free walking tours, so call for the schedule.

Inside, the building is a small, empty cylinder, with a spiral staircase snaking up to the observation deck. A tiny parapet runs around the outside and you can walk on it, making sure to hold small hands firmly—the breezes are much brisker than you'd expect. Safely down, go and read the nearby plaque, which celebrates the efforts of children all over the country to save the lighthouse when, in 1951, the Coast Guard planned to demolish it; apparently, the children's distress managed to soften even the stony heart of Robert Moses, who was Parks Commissioner at the time.

Be warned. There isn't anything in the way of an amenity here—no food concessions, no public bathrooms. But if you come up on **Little Red Lighthouse Day**, you'll find a bustling scene. This event takes place annually in the fall, and it has real local support. A stage is set up for bluegrass singers, storytellers, and sea-shanty types; rangers stand good-naturedly around venerable boats once used on the

Hudson; and earnest people at folding tables will hand you litera-
ture about ways to insure the future well-being of the Hudson.

The kids will love the Noc-Hockey and Ping-Pong tables, the
horse-drawn-wagon rides, face-painting, barbecued hamburgers,
and locally caught bluefish—grilled and presented on toothpicks.

Having come this far, treat yourself to **The Cloisters**,
which is in Fort Tryon Park, only about 15 blocks north of here. (And
if you haven't picnicked, the Fort Tryon Cafe has simple fare that
will renew flagging spirits.) Once there, head directly for the Unicorn
Tapestries. The drama and the mystery of this woven narrative
crosses generations effortlessly. The knights' sarcophagi will prove
to the children that there really were such people as knights. In the
Treasury, seek out the illuminated manuscripts, and the 16th-centu-
ry rosary bead carved from boxwood. The size of a walnut, it opens
like a locket and has unfolding panels that form a triptych depicting
scenes from the life of Christ. The detail is incredible, literally hun-
dreds of minute figures are carved into this bead, complete with
facial expressions, fingernails, and hair.

Next, stroll around the enclosed gardens, the cloisters themselves. The bare stone rooms and gloomy staircases right off the
gardens are perfect for a quick round of fantasy play, because no
matter how earnestly you explain what a cloistered monastery
means, your kids will feel that this is a castle and act accordingly. If
you all go stand on the parapet, with its brilliant views, you might
think you're in a castle too.

Little Red Lighthouse, Fort Washington Park at 181st St.
Call Urban Park Rangers at (800) 201-PARK to find out when the
lighthouse is open and the day of the festival. They will also be
happy to send you listings of all their free walks in whatever boroughs you request.
The Cloisters, Fort Tryon Park 923-3700, http://www.metmuse-
um.org/collections/department.asp?dep-7

Getting there:

1. To the Little Red Lighthouse by car and foot: Go north on the Drive to the bridge exit, then follow the signs to 178th Street. Turn left (under the bridge approach) when you can, go up to 181st Street and turn left again. Park as far west as you can. Walking west, you'll see the uptown leg of the Drive and a footbridge crossing it. Take the bridge and continue bearing left, downhill, toward the bridge.

2. To the lighthouse by subway: Take the A train to 181st Street and walk west until you see the uptown leg of the Drive. Then follow directions as above.

3. Going on to The Cloisters by car: Continuing from Fort Washington Park, drive north on the Henry Hudson Parkway. A sign will direct you to the museum's small parking lot.

4. Going on to The Cloisters by subway: Walk back along 181st Street to the subway stop, then take the A train to 190th Street, leave the station via the elevator, and walk up through Fort Tryon Park.

P.S. The bus. If you've got the time and the temperament, substitute a leisurely bus ride for the subway home. The M4 bus goes from The Cloisters all the way down upper Broadway, crossing east on 110th Street and continuing down Fifth Avenue. Stare out the windows at the absorbing, changing cityscape before you.

* *

Three Cheers for Pooh! For Who? For Pooh:
A visit to the actual *Winnie-the-Pooh* and friends with a side-trip to the *American Folk Art Museum* and/or the *Sony Wonder Technology Lab*, and *burgers* or *smoothies* for sustenance.

Winnie-the-Pooh. The very name retains its hold over even the most determinedly current child. Take yours upstairs at the **Donnell Library** on 53rd Street to see the actual, original **Winnie-the-Pooh** toys that once belonged to A. A. Milne's son

Christopher (aka Christopher Robin), and which inspired the illustrator E. H. Shepard. Seventy years old, dilapidated, and loved-to-death, the original Eeyore, Tigger, Piglet, Kanga, and, of course, the divine Pooh, still have soul. You'd recognize them anywhere; you'll want to take them home. People around the world have somehow learned that these animals are in New York; they make pilgrimages to see them and write heartfelt messages in the visitors' book. You will, too.

And now you're right across the street from the **Museum of Modern Art**—or you would be if it wasn't currently nestled into temporary quarters in Queens (see page 84), scheduled to return in 2005. Sitting in a vertical sliver of space next door is the brand-new **American Folk Art Museum**, where the human urge toward self-expression is vividly displayed. There's a snake made of bottlecaps and a tree covered in buttons, masses of duck decoys both sleek and tubby, as well as whirligigs, birdcages, spooky apocalyptic paintings, quilts (of course), and a model of the Empire State Building made of small interlocking wooden pieces, none of them glued. Colorful and passionately executed, these objects will grab your children's attention.

The cafeteria isn't suitable for the young set so after you've visited the gift shop (old-style toys at reasonable prices) steer everyone over to a restaurant. There are two branches of **Burger Heaven**, a New York institution, close by. If the little ones are intimidated by the chunky, flavorful burgers, they can find more appropriately sized grilled cheese, hot dogs, lasagna, baked potatoes, etc. on the menu.

Get takeout and you can perch on iron chairs in the vest-pocket park next door, which has a graffiti-

inspired mural, or in **Paley Park** (at 3 E. 53rd St.), which has a waterfall. Both are oases, New York City–style.

Now that you've got your energy back, it's time for some inter-activity. Head over to the **Sony Wonder Technology Lab** in Sony Plaza on Madison Avenue, where children seven or eight and up can mess around on the cutting edge of communications by working some very fancy machines—and for free! The exhibit, located in Sony Plaza, is sleek and futuristic; a friendly robot and his human helpers will direct you to a glass elevator that zooms up four floors from the atrium and deposits you at the lab. Next, you have to log in, which you do by recording your name, image, and voice; then you use a little key card to get access to the machines. All this procedural stuff will deeply impress the kids, and this is before you've even really started! As for the machines, you can play recording engineer as you tinker with the mix for a music tape, see how medical imaging works, work robots, play video games, use sound and light special effects, and so on. It's all very clear and orderly; you just pick your machine, sit down, and log in. And at the end you get a graduation certificate with your name, picture, and list of accomplishments on it. This is a very busy place teeming with school groups (they take precedence in the mornings) so you will have to show up early to get tickets and then may find yourself waiting with a snack in the light-filled, bustling atrium. You can buy all kinds of smoothies, from the weird to the wonderful, at the **C'est Bon Café** next door, as well as sandwiches, pastries, and salads. And, inevitably, there's a branch of **Starbucks** in the Sony Style store where you can buy cookies for the kids and pricey coffee for the adults. Or, if you've planned ahead (we have heard of people who are that well-organized) you could settle everybody down with a picnic from home and finish with ice cream. Whatever you choose, you'll find this a pleasant place for some serious people-watching.

Donnell Library Center (Children's Room), 20 W. 53rd St. bet. 5th and 6th Aves. 621-0636, www.nypl.org/branch/central_units/d/donnell.html

American Folk Art Museum, 45 W.43rd St. bet. 5th and 6th Aves. 265-1040, www.folkartmuseum.org

Burger Heaven, 9 E. 53rd St. bet 5th and 6th Aves., 486-2290; also at 536 Madison Ave.bet 53rd and 54th Sts., 685-6250

Museum of Modern Art, 11 W. 53rd St. bet. 5th and 6th Aves. 708-9400, www.moma.org/

Dosanko, 423 Madison Ave. bet. 48th and 49th Sts. 688-8575

Sony Wonder Technology Lab, Sony Plaza, 550 Madison Ave. bet. 55th and 56th Sts. 833-8100, www.sonywondertechlab.com/

C'Est Bon Café, 11 E. 55th St., bet. Madison Ave. and 5th Aves. 319-6680

Getting there: E or V train to Fifth Ave.

* *

Guardian of the Bay:
Harbor defense, sea breezes, and (maybe) a ghost named George at Staten Island's Fort Wadsworth.

Take the soaring Verrazzano Narrows Bridge from Brooklyn to Staten Island and far below you, tucked away at the foot of the Staten Island end, there's a fort. One of the oldest military installations in the country, and certainly one of the most exciting to visit, Fort Wadsworth is the perfect mix of crumbly, atmospheric ruin and imposing stone fortification, with grassy, breezy hillsides where everyone can decompress while inhaling the stiff sea breezes.

For years, the fort was in bad shape, and many of its old structures were abandoned; its restoration began once it became part of the National Park System in 1995. Today, much of the 220-acre site is open for visitors. You and yours can take the self-guided tour at your own pace, checking out abandoned gun batteries half-hidden

in the undergrowth. Be sure to pause at the Overlook for a spectacular view of the Upper and Lower New York Bays. For a look at things that are off-limits to the casual explorer, join one of the guided tours that start from the Visitor's Center, three blocks inside the Bay Street Gate on the left. There's also a 12-minute film shown here, recommended for ages eight and up, that makes a good preface to the tour.

Wadsworth was part of New York's complex defense system for more than 150 years. Unlike Fort Hamilton, its counterpart across the water in Bay Ridge, Wadsworth has no soldiers on the premises, but makes up for it with cool stuff. The oldest building is the massive Battery Weed, which was begun in 1847. Right at the water's edge, it's a looming stone structure with three levels of cannon-ports (space for 116 of the big guns) and great echoes. The guide will explain how cannons worked in a way that you can all understand, and he'll lead you off to see the 19th-century latrine and make ghoulish jokes for the kids. Legend has it that there are hidden tunnels and passageways between the gun emplacements.

On top of the hill sits Fort Tompkins, the barracks, where about 600 soldiers were housed. Here, you'll thread your way through so many identical, cool, vaulted-brick passageways that you'll feel as if you're in a maze. This impregnable-seeming place has two sets of walls (the granite outer walls are four feet thick and more than 30 feet high) with a space in between where attackers could be trapped in a crossfire; the guide will point out that the rifle slits in each wall are "offset"—that is, not placed directly opposite each other, to minimize the risk of shooting a comrade by accident. On our first trip, our guide encouraged us to linger in the pitch-black powder magazine, where gunpowder was stored in utter darkness, the better to protect it from sparks. The room, he informed the rapt children in our group, contained a ghost named George. George was shy that day, fortunately.

Save some time after the tour for exploring; you'll find great surprises along the trails—an observation post with a rusty phone installation from which the officers could track cannonfire and phone in course corrections; the burned-out railhead where mines were unloaded. The lighthouse is open to the public and there's a handsome row of officer's houses. If you go in the spring, wildflowers will be blooming in the woods. Bring a picnic.

Fort Wadsworth, Gateway National Recreation Area
South end of Bay Street, Staten Island, 718-354-4500, http://www.nps.gov/gate

Getting there: By car, cross the Verrazzano Bridge, lower level, take Bay St.exit, turn right and keep going. Or take the Staten Island Ferry and, at the St. George Terminal, the S51 bus.

* *

Ah, Staten Island!:
Snug Harbor with its Children's Museum, the Staten Island Zoo, the Alice Austen House, and supper overlooking the Kill Van Kull.

Much of Staten Island is a best-kept secret. In theory, therefore, you should use any excuse to ride the **Staten Island Ferry**. In practice, though, you might find yourself dawdling on arrival, since Staten Island public transportation, particularly on the weekends, is a sleepy affair. So, either go by car or bring something for the children to play with while you're waiting. You'll feel that you've left the city as you drive along quiet streets with frame houses, and tidy lawns, masses of utility wires overhead, and corner pizza parlors. Your focus will be either the **Snug Harbor Cultural Center** (which incorporates a children's museum) or the zoo. You could accomplish both, but then you'll miss out on the small town feeling of the island.

The **Snug Harbor** estate was built in the 1830s by a reformed pirate as a safe haven for retired mariners. He chose a site on a hill overlooking the waters of the Kill Van Kull, with a sweeping view of Manhattan. The buildings are a glorious mix of grand cream-colored Greek Revival buildings with colonnaded facades (these buildings contain dormitories, mess halls, meeting halls) and fairy tale–like dormered cottages where the staff lived. Much of this is open to the public, including the Newhouse Galley, with its jewel-like stained glass seascapes of lighthouses and ships.

Although the ghosts of the old salts still seem to roam the grounds, they have to share them with a cultural/artistic center. Large, inviting-looking sculptures dot the lawns and loom under the trees; the giant wooden grasshopper is excellent for climbing. Children love the spaciousness—80 acres with lawns, a duck pond, and serious Victorian gardens. But their special interest will be the **Children's Museum**, a small, hands-on, brightly colored place with a focus on bugs, as well as a number of artists' installations. These are distinctly kid-friendly, designed to have small persons walk through, touch, or peer into them. Even the smallest kids will be comfortable here, sloshing around in the water play area while their older siblings exclaim over the live, dead, and outsize grubs upstairs. Weather permitting, the gardens are great for picnicking. Failing that, check out Melville's Cafe, where they serve plain food—soups, sandwiches, bagels, hot dogs, and the like.

The **Staten Island Zoo** feels like a well-planned, small-town zoo. Ride a pony, check out the porcupines, and feed the cows and ducks while hoping that the restless goats will stage a breakout (it happens). The surprising highlight is the reptile house. It's large, dim, and very well-stocked with turtles, snakes both vast and tiny, sharks and rays, iguanas and lizards, and of course fishes—loads of fishes. It's all on a scale that children are happy with—no lines, no jostling. Adequate snacks (taco chips, hot dogs, animal crackers, etc.) can be eaten at outside tables, and the gift shop is small and inviting.

While you're on the island, don't miss another of its amazing views—this time, from the ***Alice Austen House***, which is right on the water on Hylan Boulevard, across the street from a hideous high-rise. Originally a simple farmhouse, it was remodeled into a pastoral fantasy cottage by Alice Austen, the Victorian photographer who inherited it. The low-ceilinged downstairs rooms are shady and intimate, and on the walls are Austen's pictures of her family and friends at picnics and tennis parties, as well as haunting shots of the view, which has certainly changed over the course of a hundred years, as you will see when you step outside onto the lawns. They slope down gently to a rocky beach, littered with city debris that will prove fascinating to the younger members. Relax, you're more likely to find worn bottle glass, driftwood, and pieces of old foam or tubing than the dreaded medical waste. Up and down, right in front of you, pass ships and tankers. To your immediate right (you certainly can't miss it) is the lofty sweep of the Verrazano-Narrows Bridge. Directly across is Brooklyn, and to your left, that inescapable Manhattan skyline. It's rare to find such a huge view in the city, rarer still to find it from the private grounds of a little white house with filigree decoration and a long Dutch roof.

You will be wilting by now, and there are a couple of McDonald's and pizza places around, but you don't have to do that. Instead, take Bay Street and then Richmond Terrace around the tip of the island and a little way past Snug Harbor. On the right, by the water, you will find ***R. H. Tugs***; although it has enough wood panelling and continental names on the menu to prompt subdued behavior in the youngest, Tugs will be more than happy to provide anybody who so desires with plain pasta, a burger, a BLT, or a big platter of French fries. The adult food is just fine. Meanwhile, the power stations and moorings of scenic Bayonne are on view just outside the big windows, as is the occasional monolithic container ship on its way up the Kill. As you eat, you can sense the workings of a still-busy harbor.

Snug Harbor Cultural Center, 1000 Richmond Terr.
718-448-2500, www.snug-harbor.org
Staten Island Children's Museum, at Snug Harbor
718-273-2060
Staten Island Zoo, 614 Broadway 718-442-3101 or 3100 (tape),
www.statenislandzoo.org
Alice Austen House, 2 Hylan Blvd. at Edgewater St. 718-816-4506
R. H. Tugs, 1115 Richmond Terr. 718-447-6369
Getting there: For the Staten Island Ferry, take the 1, 9, N, or R train to South Ferry and follow the signs (call 718-815-BOAT for schedules).

By bus: For Snug Harbor, the S40 from the Staten Island Ferry; for the zoo, the S48 to Broadway, then walk three blocks; for the Alice Austen House, the S51 to Bay St./Hylan Blvd.; for R. H. Tugs, the S40, a few blocks from Snug Harbor.

By car: Verrazano-Narrows Bridge (lower level), to first exit on Bay St., for Snug Harbor and Alice Austen House. Clove Rd. exit for the zoo.

* *

Shhh, Voices Carry:
The Whispering Gallery
at Grand Central Station
and other terminal delights.

After years of renovation, New York's magnificent railroad portal is a destination in itself, full of sights, shops, and great food. First, take in Grand Central's mighty Main Concourse, with its creamy marble and sweeping staircases. Look up at the beloved zodiac ceiling, now a cleaner, subtler shade of sea-blue than it's been in years. Grab a free map of the station from the information kiosk and take in the shops that line the corridors off the concourse. In the Shuttle Passage, you'll find a Discovery Channel Store (plenty of worthy toys here; we like the inflatable sharks, foam gliders, and—our favorite—the rubber alligator snout for $2.50). Right next door is the Transit Museum Gallery and Shop, where a couple of truly awesome train layouts are in motion all day. There's great stuff here: chocolate tokens (real ones, too), groovy T-shirts and, for you, subway map shower curtains and at least one book you can't live without, *Subway Cars of the BMT*. In the Lexington Passage, there's the Kids' General Store (sock monkeys, Mayan blocks, origami) and a Godiva Chocolate shop. The Grand Central Market overflows with choice meat, fish, and produce, which will probably remind the kids that they're hungry. But first things first.

Walk down one level until you're just outside the entrance to the **Oyster Bar & Restaurant**, where three beautifully tiled and vaulted corridors meet. Stand at the corners of the intersection, diagonally across from each other, and take turns speaking softly and directly into the wall. The person across the way will hear every word you say. Amazing! The same effect occurs in the excellent Oyster Bar too, which means that you can hear people across the room more clearly than those sitting next to you. The kids will probably be happier eating at the Dining Concourse, one more level down, which has an amazing range of fast food: Jamaican patties, Two Boots pizza, Knödel assorted weiners, Chinese, Japanese, Mexican, Kosher. For dessert, there's Custard Beach, the Little Pie

Company, and cheesecake from Junior's.

   P.S. **The Municipal Arts Society** has a fascinating free weekly tour of the station every Wednesday at 12:30 P.M. It's not designed for young children, but your pre-teen or teenager with a special interest in architecture or the history of New York, will love it. Colorful factoids abound. Did you know that if you were to roll a ball down from the main entrance, it wouldn't stop until it reached the trains? The highlight of the tour is a walk across one of the "skybridges," narrow passages inside the high windows that dominate the sides of the building. The public is not permitted in here; the scurrying figures in the concourse below don't even notice you four floors above them, walking between walls of glass. It's an unforgettable experience.

Grand Central Terminal, E. 42nd St. at Park Ave. 340-2710, www.grandcentralterminal.com
Municipal Arts Society, 935-3960, http://www.mas.org/
Getting there: the 4,5,6,7, or S train to Grand Central

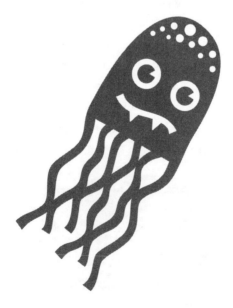

Fabulous Festivals:
Unusual celebrations,
from Native American Powwows
to Tibetan Day on Staten Island, and
fresh ways to celebrate the old reliables,
such as *Independence Day* and *Christmas.*
These outings may be slightly removed from your natural
habitat. But be bold and try them; they're winners.

Independence Night in Greenpoint

Bored on the Fourth of July? Try taking in the Macy's fireworks display. In Greenpoint. Greenpoint? Isn't that upstate? A savings bank? You want me to take my family to Greenpoint? Trust us when we say: You can do this.

Greenpoint (or Greenpernt, as it's spoken) is at the northwestern tip of Brooklyn. It's full of Russians, Poles, and artsy types who've drifted over from Williamsburg and Long Island City. Its special secret: the piers, mementos of a bustling waterfront, are directly across from the fireworks barge and much less crowded than the FDR Drive.

Not that you'll be in solitude. If you drive, leave plenty of time to park. Or take the subway; you'll get there faster and have a little time to stroll the streets. Besides, how often in your life do you get to take the G train? (You've heard of it, haven't you? Take the E or the F to Queens Plaza and transfer, or the L—the L!—to Metropolitan Avenue and transfer. Truly, you can do this.)

Stay on the G until Greenpoint Avenue. Walk east on Greenpoint (you won't be alone) until you dead-end on West Street. The piers are here; turn right and go up three blocks until you come to India Street. Everybody's turning left. You should, too. The pier in front of you has the ideal mix of location, location, and location. The crowd is rowdier than Manhattan's but utterly benign; a lot of Russians and Poles are very happy to be here on July 4th and want to tell you about it. There are zillions of children and the view is almost as good as you'd get on television. But you're not watching television; you're in Greenpoint!

P.S. There's plenty of pizza and fast food around, as well as the Polska Restaurant, 136 Greenpoint Avenue, near Manhattan Avenue (718-389-8368), which serves huge helpings of homemade food from the old country in a clean and friendly setting. But by the time the fireworks are over, the hour and the generally overwhelming air of July 4th merrymaking make the best choice just gettin' home. After all, you've got a trip ahead of you; you're in Greenpoint.

Old Home Day at Historic Richmond Town, 441 Clarke Avenue, Staten Island 718-351-1611, www.historicrichmondtown.org/

This autumn extravaganza is held on the third Sunday in October at New York's answer to Williamsburg, Virginia, Staten Island's Historic Richmond Town. The village, a couple of dozen houses in various stages of restoration spread over what was once the provincial heart of Staten Island, is worth a visit at any time, but it's particularly jolly at this time of year. All the buildings are open, and friendly locals clad in period dress stroll the village streets, sit in front parlors, and demonstrate traditional crafts and trades. A gent in buckskins demonstrates the action on a muzzle-loading rifle he seems to have built by himself, or at least been heavily involved with. All the guides have a thorough knowledge of their subjects, from tinsmithing to soldiering and caning. Even if they are, in fact, struggling actors, they have real gravity and poise. You can buy hearth-prepared soup, bread, and sarsaparilla at the tavern, right near the roof-raising demo site. The Home Brewers of Staten Island are allowed to sell their root beer but not their more serious beverages, alas. They'll give you a little cup of beer, porter, or stout for free, though. A mesmerizing model train setup occupies most of the second floor of the Court House, whose vertiginous front steps are the staging area for bluegrass, harpsichord, and choir performances. There are free buggy rides and a great mound of hay for kids to jump into. As the light starts to fade, mosey down to the gristmill and watch it actually mill grist, then see if there are any ducks left on the pond behind.

If you haven't filled up on Colonial soup, there are plenty of likely restaurants on Hylan Boulevard, the long commercial strip you'll travel to get home by car. (If you've chosen the ferry, the S74 is the bus you'll need.)

Tibetan Festival at the Jacques Marchais Museum of Tibetan Art, 338 Lighthouse Avenue, Staten Island 718-987-3500, www.tibetanmuseum.com/

The Tibetan Museum is a calm, secluded gallery, built in the style of a Tibetan mountain temple on the side of a steep hill overlooking terraced gardens, a lily pond with fish in it, and a distant view of Lower New York Bay. This little gem is open from April to November and we highly recommend it for anyone in need of an island of tranquility and willing to go to Staten Island for it.

But the time to take your kids is in the fall, for the Tibetan Festival. The mood is serene as ever, but there's also a blast of activity. Kids can cut out and color paper mandalas or yaks. There's an ancient-seeming, and artful, puppet show that you may, unbelievably enough, be able to bear watching with your children. Artisans and dealers sell Tibetan art (some quite gorgeous and expensive) and not-so-Tibetan wares in the garden, and your kids will actually enjoy some of the Tibetan food buffet (truly—the bread is soft and flat, something like a pita, and the vegetable dumplings are mild and savory). The one-room museum is dimly lit and atmospheric. It holds a three-tiered altar with gleaming figures in gold, silver, and bronze; many intricate carvings and a ceremonial apron made entirely of human bone; and a chart called the "Histomap of Religion: The Story of Man's Search for Spiritual Unity." Your little ones will be impressed, most of all with the monks—four rapt men in saffron robes who chant and ring little bells for hours on end. The spell they cast is palpable; whether you're a believer or not, a child or an adult, the sound is balm for the soul. (Just over four miles past Richmond Town, the Tibetan Museum can also be reached by the S74 bus from the Staten Island Ferry.)

The Christmas Lights of Dyker Heights

This comfortable, largely Italian neighborhood overlooks the Verrazano-Narrows Bridge and Gravesend Bay. Many of its homes are palaces, representing a wide range of architectural traditions, from antebellum Southern to Tudor and ranch. During the holiday season, houses here both large and small are tricked out in the most extravagant Christmas decorations seen outside of Rockefeller Center. Yards teem with light-encrusted trees, Nativity scenes, and life-sized Santas in sleds with reindeer in full flight. Flotillas of exuberant elves and masses of gingerbread men crowd each other right up to the property lines. The most elaborate decorations are on display from 79th to 86th Streets, between 11th and 13th Avenues. The indispensable block is 84th between 12th and 13th, where one home, called "Santa's House," features a row of elves making nutcrackers,

Mrs. Claus rocking in her chair, and a smiling, waving Winnie-the-Pooh. Across the street is a colonnaded mansion in front of which toy soldiers 12 feet high slowly stride in unison, while around them life-size dancing figures cavort in peasant fustian. Over on 82nd Street, at No. 1054, Santa sits in the picture window, tickling the ivories of a grand piano. At 86th Street and 12th Avenue, more massive wooden soldiers. By the end of your drive, you'll consider yourself lucky to be getting away with an adequately bedecked tree and the odd sprig of holly around the living room. Afterwards, take everybody out for some old-fashioned Italian food at L&B Spumoni Gardens, a family-style restaurant at 2725 86th Street (718-372-8400). P.S. A car is best for this, but you can take the M train (rush hour) or the W to 79th Street or 18th Avenue. Bring trail mix.

The Dig-Your-Own Christmas Tree and Free-Range Reindeer Farm

A tree farm grows in Jersey, but right now we're not sure where. **The Hazienda** in Holmdel, N.J., an institution where you could always find beautiful trees, warm spirits, cocoa and free-roaming reindeer, has moved. According to the owners, you will still be able to buy pre-cut trees, have one specially cut for you, or cut your own (bring tools) at their new location, which will be near the old one. Call 732-450-0666 or visit www.thehaziendaplantation.com for more information.

The New York Turtle and Tortoise Society Show

If you're contemplating buying one of those silver-dollar-sized turtles you saw for sale in Chinatown (see page 30), why not attend this show, held every spring in a school playground in the West Village? That's where you'll see just how imposing your little green friend might become. If you're just curious about these mysterious charmers, you won't be disappointed. Some of the more gigantic beasts roam free, munching on stuff, while others lie snug as kittens against their owners' chests; everywhere turtle-lovers are enthusiastically swapping tips about health, hygiene, and diet. This placid scene is a sweet example of the eccentricities of the human heart. For the New York Turtle and Tortoise Show, check www.nytts.org

Native American Powwows

Two or three times a year, representatives from tribes across the country (as well as Central and South America) gather somewhere in the metropolitan area to compete in dancing, chanting, and drumming; sell their craftwork; and raise public consciousness of their tribal identities. Powwows are great fun, especially the dancing. This begins after the drummers establish a groove and the chanters set up their hypnotic drone; men, women, and children circle, shuffle, and leap while the drummers begin to improvise, sitting in a huddle and taking their cues from each other. The sounds and the swirling feathers and buckskin are thrilling; children will realize immediately that this is the real thing. Don't miss the crafts, such as beaded belts, real (toy) spears, or bows and arrows made of wood by real tribespeople. And try the food—everything from excellent buffalo burgers, chili, and Indian tacos to frybread sprinkled with powdered sugar. Powwows of various sizes are held all over the city. The largest and most impressive is the Gateway to the Nations, which is sometimes held at Fort Hamilton in Bay Ridge, Brooklyn. For locations, consult the Red Hawk Indian Arts Council's website (http://redhawkarts.home. mindspring.com) or call its office at 718-686-9297.

Clearwater's Great Hudson Revival

On Father's Day weekend, when you're looking for something special to do, take the car (or rent one) and drive up the Hudson to Clearwater's Great Hudson Revival, which takes place over two days. Started in the late 1960s by folksinger Pete Seeger and dedicated to preserving the delicate ecosystem of the Hudson River, this lovely event is relaxed, old-timey, and welcoming. The festival is now held next to the river at Croton Point Park, about an hour and 45 minutes from the city. On several stages, many performers—some of the stature of Arlo Guthrie or Bonnie Raitt—do their stuff, everything from zydeco or jazz to opera. You can sample ethnic foods and buy crafts. For the children, there's a special area with crafts and activities, a children's stage, storytellers, jugglers, clowns, magicians, and mimes. Pete Seeger himself, that venerable sprite, may even be beaming from behind a microphone somewhere. So go, have fun, and do something to save our waters. Call 845-454-7673 or visit www.clearwater.org/ for details.

Chapter Four
Cityscapes:
All Around the Town

You Must Take the N train:

(to Queens), where you'll find the **Socrates Sculpture Park** (for art you can climb on), the **Museum of the Moving Image** (for Mesozoic video games), **MoMA** (for awhile, anyway), the **Omonia Cafe, Uncle George's, Tierras Colombianas,** and more (for delectable food).

A relatively small area of Queens, comprising parts of Long Island City and Astoria, has gone from cultural outpost to hub in a remarkably short time. There's enough to see and do here to justify several trips, but if you have nice weather, start by taking the N train to Broadway in Astoria, then walking west toward Vernon Boulevard and the East River. The dense commercial traffic gives way to residential streets and then warehouses.

Ahead of you, at the water's edge, is **Socrates Sculpture Park**, almost five acres of not-at-all-manicured shorefront littered with a jumble of contemporary sculpture and set against views of the river, Roosevelt Island, and the Upper East Side. It is one of 14 "designated pedestrian sites" in New York and the city's most unusual picnic spot. Founded by sculptor Mark di Suvero in the 1980s as an informal gallery for local artists, the park has been bought by the city, which put up a plaque and, fortunately, left it at that.

The art here changes twice a year and its quality varies widely. But Socrates Park has a feature that lifts it above all competition for kids' interest: not one of the works on display here is off-limits. They can all be touched, sat on, ridden, rubbed, or run around. Indeed, many seem designed for hands-on use. As of this writing, your children can climb on an enormous green tree snake, run on a caged-in catwalk which surrounds four saplings, enter a steep brick amphitheater built inside a hill, or buddy up to a trio of larger-than-life teenagers on pedestals. Eat your picnic while relaxing in a nicely squishy-looking sofa made of mosaic tile.

Check out the fenced-off area diagonally across from the park's main entrance, the one that's patrolled by dogs (don't worry, it's a sturdy fence). With luck, you'll see sculptors in hard hats using cranes and other enormous contraptions to assemble monumental works-in-progress. Elsewhere, young artists with their kids chat with friends and chisel marble between sips of coffee.

If it's not picnic weather, walk or take the Q104 bus back down Broadway, and you'll soon be in the heart of New York's Greek-est neighborhood. Try **Uncle George's**, which looks like your standard coffee shop—except for the lamb roasting on a spit in the window and the more-esoteric-than-usual Greek specialties on the lengthy menu. Close by, but an ethnic world away, is **Tierras Colombianas**, where you can get rice and beans, fried chicken, and other Latin specialties that small mouths enjoy. Where ever you go, save room for dessert and proceed to the **Omonia Cafe** on the corner of Broadway and 33rd Street. Here you can drink serious coffee and sample the rice pudding while the children put away lavish sundaes or gaudy, sticky cake—a favorite is the chocolate cake topped with an icing mouse.

Fortified, stagger another few blocks to the **American Museum of the Moving Image**, which houses all manner of movie tchotchkes—set models and drawings, costumes, hair and makeup samples from *Planet of the Apes*, *Amadeus*, and the like, as well as exhibits explaining animation and special effects. In Tut's Movie Palace, a tiny (36 seats), riotously kitschy movie theater designed by Red Grooms, the kids can see classic serials from the golden age of film.

The unchallenged kids' favorite at AMOMI is the hands-on video game exhibit. They're all here: Donkey Kong, Pac-Man, and such cult classics as Star Wars, Karate Champ, Pole Position, and Space Invaders. Most are in working order and each has a card explaining its role in the saga of computer-operated entertainment. You'll use a lot of change, but save some for the gift shop. It's a good one: not just the usual logoed mugs and T-shirts and caps, but also posters, fridge magnets, claymation sets, and lunch bags of undeniable adorability.

Even in smaller, temporary quarters in Queens, the **Museum of Modern Art**'s collection—from austere furniture to colorful canvases by all the modern masters, plus the occasional shiny vehicle or toaster—is a blast for all. If it's been a while since you've looked at Van Gogh's *Starry Night* or the Cezanne *Bather* in the flesh, do yourself a favor.

For arty kids, there's another option nearby: the temporary home of the **Noguchi Museum**. Its permanent home, only a few blocks from Socrates Park, is closed for renovation until 2003. This artist's work may be familiar to the kids from his many public works. Everything here is spare, abstract, and so tactile you'll want to reach out and handle it. Resist the temptation; touching is not permitted because, as a guide explains, the natural oils in our hands are bad for the stone.

American Museum of the Moving Image, 3601 35th Ave. bet. 36th and 37th Sts., Astoria 718-784-0077, www.ammi.org/

The Isamu Noguchi Museum, 36-01 43rd Avenue at 36th Street, Long Island City, Queens, New York, 718-204-7088, www.noguchi.org/

Museum of Modern Art, 33 Street at Queens Blvd. Long Island City, Queens (212) 708-9400, www.moma.org

Socrates Sculpture Park, Broadway at the East River, 718-956-1819, www.socratessculpturepark.org/

Uncle George's, Broadway at 34th St. 718-626-0593

Tierras Colombianas, 33-01 Broadway at 33rd St., 718-956-3012

Omonia Cafe, Broadway at 33rd St. 718-274-6650

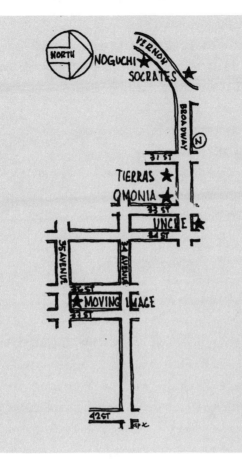

Getting there:

For **Socrates Sculpture Park**, N train to Broadway in Astoria, Queens

For **MoMA:** 7 Local to 33rd Street, Queens

On weekends, a shuttle bus runs between MoMA's Manhattan and Queens locations. In Queens, shuttles go between MoMA and other Queens destinations, including the Noguchi Museum. Call (212) 708-9750 or visit www.queensartlink.org for more information.

Brooklyn-by-the-Sea:
The *New York Aquarium,*
Coney Island, Nathan's fries (sigh!),
Brighton Beach, Mrs. Stahl's Knishes.

This is a big and busy trip, so prepare for a long day. Since the **Aquarium** draws a crowd year-round, it's best to get to this marvelous place situated right on the boardwalk early in the morning, when you can commune privately with the sharks without getting run over by countless little stroller wheels. There's a lot to see: the family of beluga whales (approach the windows quietly so as not to frighten the babies); endearing walruses, seals, otters, and penguins at the Sea Cliffs; exhibits of river and shore life; and giant rays, eels, and squid. Call to find out about feeding times and special events. The food available for humans is adequate, but it would be much more fun to go right to **Coney Island**, just a few blocks west along the boardwalk.

The whole area is terminally decrepit and funky now, but the intermingled smells of fried food, suntan oil, and the sea are truly seductive, as is the mix of old-timers, young families out for the day, and expressionless hipsters all in black, smoking on the street corners. The police are discreet but ubiquitous, so you can feel safe. But make sure you're gone by sundown, when a less amiable mix arrives on the scene.

Coney Island's Astroland rides are thrilling for the younger set and safe enough for their parents' peace of mind. (But beware the deceptively tame-looking Tilt-A-Whirl. While your children are demanding their second and third turns, you might be parked on a nearby bench, head wedged miserably between your knees.) Bigger kids can brave whatever you will permit, from the Cyclone roller coaster to the Wonder Wheel or the enormous ship that swings sickeningly from side to side, high above the crowds. You can look nostalgically around at the sites of Dreamland and Steeplechase.

The mighty Thunderbolt rollercoaster (complete with the little cottage underneath, immortalized by Woody Allen in *Annie Hall*) is gone. In its place stands KeySpan Park, home of our new local heroes, the **Brooklyn Cyclones**. But a few relics of the old days remain, like the B&B Carousell [sic], almost hidden under the elevated train tracks across Surf Ave. This carousel is tattier than others you'll find in the city (see page 126), but unlike those, it still has brass rings to grab if you lean out far enough as you go whirling around.

One of Coney Island's most interesting attractions goes by the name of Dick Zigun. He runs an exuberantly weird boardwalk freak show called **Sideshows by the Seashore**, and is the driving force behind the raucous (and ever-groovier) Mermaid Day Parade, and also the New Year's Day Polar Bears event at which assorted doughty souls, many of them Russian, jump into the frigid sea. On summer weekends, Sideshows runs almost continuously, affording your children a rare chance to see a sword-swallower, a fire-eater, a snake-charmer, and other specialists at a reasonable cost. Afterwards, you can visit Zigun's "museum" full of decrepit Coney Island memorabilia.

Snacks are everywhere, of course—at **Nathan's** (good dogs, the world's best French fries) and on the boardwalk. There's even a McDonald's, if you must. Don't hesitate on the question of cotton candy—going home with a sticky chin is part of the deal.

You're not going home yet. Instead, stroll back down to the boardwalk and along, sniffing the sea air, maybe going down to the sand to dip a toe in the water. End up at **Brighton Beach**, which is now an affluent Russian village. See how long it takes your children to notice that nobody around them is speaking English. Gape at the old-country delicacies, caviar and sturgeon, black bread, and preserves. The prices are good if you want to stock up.

See who can be the first to spot graffiti in Cyrillic script. And then, when everyone is truly starving, tackle a knish from **Mrs. Stahl's**, on Brighton Beach Avenue. They come in flavors—boy, do they ever! From cabbage to mushroom, by way of potato, kasha, apple, and onion. Do not underestimate the ability of an adolescent to scarf these down. Buy in bulk and then slump contentedly on the subway all the way home.

New York Aquarium, Surf Ave. at W. 8th St. 718-265-3474, wcs.org/home/zoos/nyaquarium
KeySpan Park, 1904 Surf Avenue, 718-449-TIXS
Brooklyn Cyclones: www.brooklyncyclones.com
Sideshows by the Seashore, 1208 Surf Ave. at W. 12th St. 718-372-5101, www.coneyislandusa.com/
Nathan's Famous Restaurant, 1310 Surf Ave. near Stillwell Ave. 718-946-2202
Mrs. Stahl's Knishes, 1001 Brighton Beach Ave. at Coney Island Ave. 718-648-0210
Getting there: Take the W to Coney Island/Stillwell Avenue. Return via the Q at Brighton Beach.

* *

Hallowed Ground:
The site of the World Trade Center, Wall Street and environs, including the Exchange, the Criminal Courts, art, history, and all kinds of bargains.

Built, along with the World Financial Center and Battery Park City, on some of the world's most expensive landfill, the World Trade Center exemplified the city's most aggressive and daring mode. It was, literally, an awesome sight. The vast construction pit it has become is also awesome, both in its physical scale and the gravity of

its atmosphere. As of this writing, the viewing area runs along one side and is not spacious. On a weekend, the wait to squeeze through can be considerable and the view less than spectacular. By all means, brave the crush if your kids are old enough to understand what they're seeing and, equally important, if they're up for it. Otherwise, spend your time here exploring the neighborhood, where New York's oldest past and most recent present coexist so dramatically.

The Marina is as beautiful as ever, with the occasional gigantic yacht moored alongside more modest vessels. So is the Winter Garden, with its towering glass roof, stately palms, and regal staircase. You're a short walk from from wonderful **Nelson Rockefeller Park** (see page 111) and the **Irish Hunger Memorial**. The latter doesn't have much in the way of explanation, but kids will enjoy walking around this miniature stoney hillside (which includes stones from each Irish county and the crumbled walls of an Irish cottage) that seems to float above the street.

The shopping is good enough down here to merit a trip by itself. Directly across the street from the WTC site is **Century 21**, the great discount department store where your Wall Street friends have been finding incredible bargains on everything from toaster ovens to Calvin Klein undies for years. Renovated since the attacks, it is, more than ever, an essential stop for budding fashionistas. Further east on Park Place sits **J&R**, another neighborhood stalwart that weathered severe damage and then vastly reduced business to remain a technogeek's paradise. Spread over several storefronts, the place offers electronic tackle of every type.

Close by is another piece of hallowed ground: the **African Burial Ground** on Reade Street, just east of 290 Broadway. There's nothing there anymore, except for a neat rectangle of green lawn, planted with shrubs, set between the huge buildings. Nonetheless, its presence is haunting, especially when you read the sign stating that 20,000 or more Africans were buried in this ground from 1629 until its closing in 1794. Continue east, to the forbidding **Criminal Courts** building on Centre Street. It's a sobering experience to tiptoe in and sit for awhile, watching the endless procession of the (mostly) disadvantaged brought up before the judicial system. The bored police officers lounging against the walls, lawyers huddling and muttering, and the stiffly upright defendants—many of whom can't understand what's being said—are, for some, a sight right out of Dickens. For your children, it's a side of New York that they may know about in theory, but have probably never seen.

One of the most spectacular sights in the Wall Street area has to be the bustling trading floor of the **New York Stock Exchange**, as seen from the visitor's gallery one floor above it. To be sure of getting a ticket for the short (30- to 45-minute) tour, show up before 11 AM (by 9, if it's a school holiday), since there will be a line for the limited number of tickets. The tour starts with a video and then, upstairs in the gallery, you can look down on the action as you listen to a taped description of what exactly all those intense-looking fellows in their colored jackets are doing. If your child has a real interest in the world's financial workings, you must book a tour of the **Federal Reserve Bank**, just a few blocks away at the junction of Liberty and Wall. This place actually issues currency, and it houses more gold than Fort Knox, five floors of it, owned by the nations of the world. In the old days, international transactions used to be marked here by the transfer of gold; it was actually trundled from one area to another. They do let you see the gold, but there are two problems with the tour—you have to book a month in advance and you have to be 16.

There's fast food everywhere, but we recommend just snacking for the sake of a special early dinner. Take a break from history with an outdoor art breather. Start with **Louise Nevelson's Shadows and Flags** sculptural installation in the plaza in front of the Federal Reserve. Look up from right in the middle of the seven jagged forms—they're designed to be viewed that way—and then cross the street, into the lower level of Chase Manhattan Plaza. You're facing a plate glass window, behind which is a characteristically discreet and meditative **Noguchi** work, a sunken garden with black rocks and lapping water. Walk past a striking car fender sculpture on the wall (*Triptych* by Jason Seeley) to the escalator, which will take you up to the outdoor plaza containing the wonderfully loony and idiosyncratic **Group of Four Trees** by Dubuffet. These looming black-and-white oddities, more mushroomy than treelike, are a charming surprise here in the stuffy ambience of high finance.

Walk across Wall Street or Exchange Place to Broadway and check out the odd gorgeous lobby or architectural detail. You could walk down to the **Cunard Building** (now a post office) at 25 Broadway, for example, which has an incredible painted ceiling, as well as murals and frescoes from the days when you could book your ticket on the Lusitania or the Titanic. Then walk up to the formidable **Trinity Church**, one of the city's richest institutions, rebuilt in its third incarnation to dominate Wall Street. (Literally—you can see it in front of you as you walk up the street.)

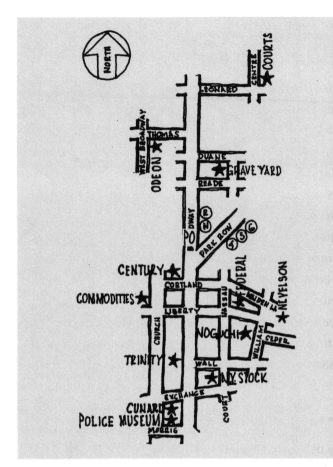

Alexander Hamilton and Robert Fulton (the steamboat man) are buried in the churchyard. By the way, it was the refusal to permit Africans to be buried here that brought the Reade Street burial ground into being.

Look down Broadway to the Battery, and you get a sense of the small scale of old New York. And start thinking about dinner. **Odeon** on West Broadway remains a favorite; it is perhaps the coolest restaurant in New York to offer a children's menu, and the food is as beguiling as the atmosphere. But there are dozens of good restaurants down here that are offering all sorts of special deals. It's a good time to experiment.

Century 21, 22 Cortlandt St. bet. Broadway and Church St. 227-9092

J&R, Park Row bet. Beekman and Ann Sts. 238-9000

African Burial Ground, Reade St., east of 290 Broadway

Criminal Courts, 100 Centre St. at Leonard St.

New York Stock Exchange, 20 Broad St. bet. Wall St. and Exchange Pl. 656-5168, www.nyse.com/

Federal Reserve Bank, 33 Liberty St. at Maiden Ln. 720-6130, www.ny.frb.org/

Louise Nevelson Plaza, William and Liberty Sts.

Noguchi and **Dubuffet**, 1 Chase Manhattan Plaza at Cedar St.

Cunard Building, U.S. Post Office (Bowling Green), 25 Broadway bet. Beaver St. and Exchange Pl. 363-9460

Trinity Church, Broadway at Wall St., 602-0872

Odeon, 145 W. Broadway at Thomas St. 233-0507

Getting there: A, C, J, M, Z, 1, 2, 3, 4, 5 to Fulton St./-Broadway-Nassau

* *

Way Down South Street:
Breakfast at **Ruben's Empanadas,** a tour of the **South Street Seaport,** and then over the **Brooklyn Bridge** to **Empire State Park,** and the **Fulton Landing,** then reward yourself with world-class pizza at **Grimaldi's Pizzaria,** plus chocolate and ice cream.

This trip requires energy and a lovely weekend day (you don't want chilly gusts off the river to buffet the smallest member). Fuel up with a flaky, savory breakfast empanada at **Ruben's** on Fulton Street. They have bacon-and-egg as well as the traditional spinach, meat and chicken versions of these savory patties. Then head down to the **South Street Seaport**, which, despite its rampant commercialism and cranked-up Ye Olde Nautical aspect, turns out to be invigorating and full of nice surprises.

Stroll old streets like Cannon's Walk and Schermerhorn Row, soaking up what's left of the 19th-century port ambience. There are Federal–era buildings on Peck Slip, between Water and Front streets, some sliding into decrepitude. The oldest is No. 273 Water Street, now a ruin but formerly the house/store that retired sea-captain Joseph Rose built for himself in 1773. Stop at the Visitors' Center at 209 Water Street, and buy a ticket that will admit you to the South Street Seaport Museum and its eight historic ships, including the venerable Peking, a cargo vessel built in 1911. (Don't miss the short film of the Peking fighting a storm.) The museum occupies several buildings, including the Whitman Gallery, which features one of the world's great collections of ocean liner models and memorabilia. There are also tours, children's activities every weekend, and plenty of special events, from Fire Day to the Festival of Maritime Work and Culture (call in advance or check the very comprehensive website to see what's on the docket).

Pier 17 isn't much different from a tacky mall anywhere in the country, only this one has a view of the Brooklyn Bridge from its third-floor food court. There's also a shop that sells only purple merchandise and another that only does butterfly motifs, not to mention Nothin' But Lids and Everything's a Lighter. And there are plenty of places to stock up on Three Stooges glassware, jokey T-shirts, and all your 'N Sync needs. Alternatively, you could just hang out, watching teenagers in billowing jeans show off their skateboard stunts for the tourists.

Now head over to the **Brooklyn Bridge**.

(Walk up Beekman Street to Park

Row, turn right, and you'll see the entrance to the walkway just across from City Hall.) It's magnificent up there, but scary, with the wind whistling through the cables and the maddened buzzing of the traffic below you. Hang on to the tinies, who should have a hat or scarf to protect their ears from the ever-present wind. Before going, look at David McCullough's *The Great Bridge*, so that you can give the kids a sense of the engineer's achievements and the odd gruesome detail (20 involved in the bridge's construction died, most from the bends, including its designer, John Roebling).

Coming down off the bridge (first exit to your left, left at the bottom of the stairs, and then left again), you'll find yourself on Fulton Street. Walk down toward the river and the bridge. Turn right under the bridge approach, then take the first left down to the water. To your right is **Empire State Park**, a hilly meadow dotted with benches, shrubbery, and plenty of sculpture. The panoramic view takes in all three of the lower Manhattan bridges to Brooklyn. Behind you are cleanly gutted warehouses— just flat floors and bare brick walls open to the sky—that cry out for a game of tag or just some running around.

The essential next stop is **Grimaldi's**, an old-style pizza parlor just up Old Fulton Street. The owner is a dapper, white-haired gent, Frank Sinatra is on the walls and in the jukebox, and the waiters are expert at swinging between the crowded tables without stepping on errant three-year-olds. The fabulous pizza is the real thing—fresh mozzarella, homemade tomato sauce, delicate smoky crust—with no goat cheese or radicchio to ruin it for the children. Grimaldi's is very popular, especially at kid-time (5:30 PM on) but the line moves fast, so stick with it. Afterwards, stroll down to the water again, this time to **Fulton Landing**, between

Bargemusic and the River Cafe. A ferry ran from here to lower Manhattan from 1814 until the 1960s. Now it has little benches and a wrought-iron fence with inscriptions from Walt Whitman, who lived close by. It also has the **Brooklyn Ice Cream Factory**, housed in the renovated Fireboat House and serving a small but scrumptious selection of ice cream delights. And speaking of delights, you can't leave without moseying down Water Street to **Jacques Torres Chocolate**. The candies here are as beautiful to look at as they are to eat. The kids will love the Classic Hot Chocolate, you'll go for the Wicked variety (it's spiced). On Saturdays, there are pastries, brownies, palmiers, and the legendary mudslide cookies.

Now flag down a taxi leaving the River Cafe or take the subway home. Either way, the kids will fall asleep en route.

Ruben's Empanadas, 64 Fulton St. near the Seaport 962-5330
South Street Seaport Museum and Visitors' Center, 209 Water Street, 748-8600. For information on family programs, call 748-8758, www.southstseaport.org/
Grimaldi's Pizza, 19 Old Fulton St. bet. Water and Front Sts. 718-858-4300
Brooklyn Ice Cream Factory at Fulton Ferry Landing Pier, 718-246-3963
Jacques Torres Chocolate, 66 Water Street, 718-875-9772, www.mrchocolate.com
Getting there: The 2, 3, 4, or 5 train to Fulton St., or the A or C to Broadway-Nassau. Walk east on Fulton St. to Water St. Returning from Brooklyn: A from High Street.

Village People and Places:
the *Union Square Greenmarket*,
the *Forbes Magazine Galleries*,
***Washington Square*,**
adorable little houses and streets,
***Li-Lac chocolates* (from heaven),**
and a restaurant with a thing about cowgirls.

The Village can be hard for kids—too crowded, too much architecture and history, too many serious restaurants. This trip, preferably undertaken on a bustling Saturday, makes it fun. Start at the **Union Square Greenmarket** so that the children can fuel up with a little bottle of fancy juice and pretzels, muffins, or the chocolate chip cookies from Wilklow Farm, which, in addition to being large, also have the preferred ratio of chips to cookie.

Stroll down Broadway. If you're feeling expansive, stop in at **Forbidden Planet** and spend a few minutes amid the pasty-faced science-fiction fanatics while your children pick over the comics, figures, games, and posters. Then go west down 12th Street and across Fifth Avenue to the **Forbes Magazine Galleries**.

This place is a joy. Malcolm Forbes never put away childish things. On the contrary, he collected and cherished them, and much of his collection is on show here—12,000 toy soldiers, Fabergé eggs, presidential memorabilia, and more. The first gallery contains 500 toy ships and boats of all sizes and degrees of complexity, deployed in tableaux on gleaming glass seas. All around, you hear jolly nautical band music and the booming of ship's horns. The submarine display is the real kid-pleaser; the subs float murkily behind a long vertical window, you hear the ominous beeping of depth finders, and suddenly you notice a model of the *Lusitania,* sprawled on the bottom.

In the next gallery, there are toy soldiers and other figures, set up in tiny tableaux. You can see a pitched battle between Aztecs

and Cortés's conquistadores, tiny wounded soldiers in field hospitals, Indians on a moving belt circling wagon trains, and regiment after regiment marching on parade. (Be warned: some of these tableaux are, incomprehensibly, too high up for children under the age of, say, eight. So you may have to hoist them up from time to time, or locate the stool that's usually somewhere around.) Don't miss the scene of William Tell preparing to shoot the apple from his son's head. Peer through a little porthole-shaped window in a room called Land of Counterpane, and you can pretend to be the child of Robert Louis Stevenson's poem, with all your soldiers laid out in formation on the bed in front of you.

Two more stops include the presidential memorabilia for a look at Abraham Lincoln's actual stovepipe hat, the eyeglasses he dropped when he was shot, and his handwritten copy of the Gettysburg Address. Last, the Fabergé room, which, though it's more enthralling for adults, has aspects that children too will find fascinating—the miniaturization, the surprises, such as hens, tucked away inside the 12 gorgeous eggs made for the czars.

Next, go down Fifth Avenue to **Washington Square**. With luck, there'll be a pleasantly ramshackle assortment of buskers, magicians, and mimes—some of whom are talented (this is where Philippe Petit, the noted high-wire artist, used to perform). If your kids have a taste for the macabre, point out the ancient Hanging Elm at the northwest corner of the park, once used for public hangings but, sadly, since 1992, missing the relevant branch.

Now for the most Villagey aspect of the tour. Walk west two

blocks, to Seventh Avenue, preferably along **Bleecker Street**. Here, in among the tourist traps, there still are rundown record stores, bakeries, and lovely old cafes with tin ceilings. West of Sixth Avenue, you'll hit the enticing Italian food shops; you owe it to yourselves to invest in bread from **Zito's**. At Seventh Avenue, turn south, and head for some of **New York's oldest, prettiest blocks**. Of course they look familiar; you've seen them in countless movies. Take a right, down St. Luke's Place to Hudson Street, then up Morton Street, then left again onto Bedford Street. Here you'll find No. 75 $\frac{1}{2}$, a house which is not merely New York's narrowest (at 9 $\frac{1}{2}$ feet), but which was also inhabited by Edna St. Vincent Millay, John Barrymore, and Cary Grant—in that order. Walk west down Commerce Street to the Cherry Lane Theater. Commerce dead-ends at Barrow Street; turn right, back toward Seventh, cross Bedford, and you'll see on your left a mysterious little stone courtyard. Walk in. Ahead of you is a forbidding, heavy barred door with no sign—swing it open and you'll find yourself in **Chumley's**, once a speakeasy and now a convivial bar with framed book jackets on the walls, a world-class jukebox (rivaled only by that in the Corner Bistro on West 4th Street), and a roaring log fire. Children are allowed to eat here; the food is eclectic and fine. But if you have more energy, go out the back entrance onto Bedford (another door without a sign), and turn right until you hit Grove Street. At the corner, gape awhile at Twin Peaks, a truly eccentric house at 102 Bedford, and at the tiny frame cottage in front of it. Then make a left and keep walking until you see another secret place— Grove Court, a perfect row of six small red houses dating from 1854, tucked away in their private courtyard.

Surfeited on architecture, the

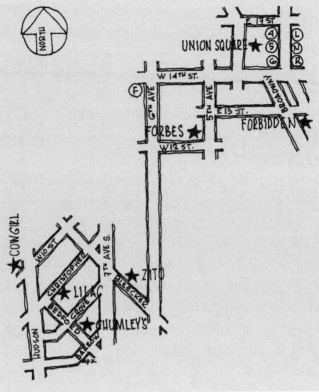

children need rewards. Take them to **Li-Lac**, the old-fashioned French chocolate shop on Christopher Street, where you can dither happily over the selection of chocolates handmade in the back room, and then think about dinner. Obviously there are masses of places to choose from—the Elephant and Castle on Greenwich Ave. at 11th Street, John's Pizzeria on Bleecker, and any number of taquerias and cafes. But, for a change, why not go for the **Cowgirl Hall of Fame** on Hudson Street? This is not one of those mass-produced margaritas-from-a-mix "concept restaurants." On the contrary, it's the personal expression of Sherry Delamarter, who is obsessed with things Western, especially cowgirls. There's a little museum in there, and a mock Western living room with a painted night sky above the roof beams; there are glass-fronted displays of barbed wire, tied by the great barbed-wire tiers of the Old West. This is definitely one woman's vision but wildly appealing to all, as is the Western-cum-Southwestern food and drink. (A special kiddie menu features not just burgers and dogs but also a single cheese enchilada, Frito pie *made in the bag,* and so on.) Everyone here is friendly; on your way out, investigate the campy little gift shop, featuring water-squirting pistols in holsters, beaded belts, bandannas, and cactus salt-and-pepper sets. Then plan to come back sometime for brunch; it's a great menu.

Union Square Greenmarket, Union Square West and 17th St.
Forbidden Planet, 840 Broadway at 13th St. 473-1576
Forbes Magazine Galleries, 62 Fifth Ave. at 12th St. 206-5548, www.ny.com/museums/forbes. magazine.galleries.html
Zito, 259 Bleecker St. bet. Sixth and Seventh Aves. 929-6139
Chumley's Restaurant, 86 Bedford St. bet. Barrow and Grove Sts. 675-4449
Li-Lac Chocolates Inc., 120 Christopher St. bet. Bleecker and Hudson Sts. 242-7374
Cowgirl Hall of Fame, 519 Hudson St. at 10th St. 633-1133
Getting there: 4, 5, 6, L, N, or R to Union Sq.; F, L, V train to 14th St.

* *

Midtown Lite:
Radio City Music Hall's tour,
fancy moviegoing at the Ziegfeld,
assorted waterfalls, and an irresistible diner.

Save this trip for a day when you're prepared to spend a bit of money to get a bit of pampering. The first stop: **Radio City Music Hall**, for a tour (which you can take any time except Christmas or Easter). It may seem corny, but people do report near-spiritual feelings at the sight of that gorgeous place up close and empty. In the course of 45 minutes, you will study Radio City's interior architecture, the Mighty Wurlitzer, the proscenium arch, the backstage areas, and the complex workings of the stage (those big gears and levers are especially thrilling for kids). Some call it a wonder of the world; you might call it $12 per adult and $6 per child well spent. Afterwards, wander over to the **Channel Gardens** (and the rink to watch the skaters if it's winter). Show the children as much of Rockefeller Center's paintings, sculpture, and architectural decoration as they will tolerate, and then take the glass-enclosed elevator down from the rink to the lower level. Children will love the ant-colony feel of the bustling concourse, and you will have many choices for food—anything from Mrs. Fields Cookies to Au Bon Pain—and souvenirs (excellent Statues of Liberty made of some green polymerlike substance on a white marblelike base).

The next luxurious stop is a movie at the **Ziegfeld Theatre**. This is excessive and thrilling in its gigantic way, with all the Dolby sound and the tall escalators and the blockbuster movies and the requisite exorbitantly priced candy, etc. It's a far cry from the local multiplex, where your feet instantly meld with the gum on the floor and you can hear the movies playing in the theaters on either side.

Next, benign and mellow, check out a couple of **waterfalls** on your way west for dinner. You may get sidetracked by the **NBA Store** (where you can play basketball arcade games and chuck actual balls through actual hoops while deciding which of the basketball-related mugs, keyrings, totes, or T-shirts to buy) but keep going and you'll hit Sixth Avenue, which, just at this point, has looming contemporary

sculptures and spectacular fountains. Most appealing for kids: the assemblage in front of the Credit Lyonnais building (between 52nd and 53rd Sts.), which combines massive green limbless figures by Jim Dine with a low fountain that flows so seamlessly and smoothly over a flat shelf that the kids won't be able to resist dabbling their fingers in the water. Head down Sixth to 49th Street and turn west along the side of the McGraw-Hill building. Just behind it, you'll see a little park—investigate and you will find yourself walking through a water tunnel, with (glass-enclosed) water cascading around your head and down beside you.

Finally, dispel whatever feelings of repose this may have engendered with a visit to **Ellen's Stardust Diner** at 51st Street and Broadway. How to explain this place? It's a fantasy of a fifties diner—all chrome and booths, with a jukebox, TV screens, and waiters in loudly patterned vests. The menu is comfort food of many lands—everything from fajitas to French fries. Your children will happily chow down on the shakes and malteds, sliders, sandwiches, or chicken potpie. Then there's the little train that goes steadily chugging high up around the perimeter. If you can manage to go there after 7 P.M. any night from Wednesday through Saturday, you'll be treated to the sight of singing waitpersons strutting their actor stuff. Oldies on the TV, maybe a lime rickey—and that train. How could you deny your kids this seminal experience?

Radio City Music Hall, 1260 Ave. of the Americas at 50th St. 632-4041, http://www.radiocity.com/

Ziegfeld Theatre, 141 W. 54th St. bet. Sixth and Seventh Aves. 505-CINE #602

NBA Store, 666 Fifth Ave. bet. 52nd and 53rd Sts., 515-6221

Ellen's Stardust Diner, 1650 Broadway at 51st St. 956-5151

Chapter Five

Action without Angst:
You Can All Join In

New York City's wonderful parks: Consider what you can do: baseball, cricket, field hockey, football, soccer, croquet, bird-watching, basketball, golf, lawn bowling, boccie, rowboating and canoeing, model-yacht sailing, nature walks, track and field, astronomy, paddle ball, cycling, curling, rollerblading, fishing, horseback riding, ice skating, wall climbing, rock climbing, and swimming. Did we mention softball, haunted walks and hayrides in season, Buddhist meditations, winter fairs, equestrian fairs, Highland games, Easter egg rolls, square dances, yoga classes, chess, checkers, children's theater, and dance? And let's not forget traditional pleasures such as feeding the ducks, rolling down hills, and picnicking. Absolutely the best way to find out what's on is to be in touch with the Urban Park Rangers. They're courteous and very knowledgable—and they send out free mailing lists. Like the parks themselves, they are a resource no parent should ever underestimate. (By the way, did we leave out free Shakespeare?) Call (800) 201-PARK or visit nycparks.completeinet.net/.

Gateway Sports Center in Brooklyn: You can reach it by public transportation, but not easily. The trip by car is worth it, especially if you're a multisport family, as Gateway offers tennis courts, batting cages with varied levels of pitching speed, a driving range, and one of the city's prettiest 18-hole miniature golf courses, with big clumps of pampas grass and a little stream. You get a great feeling of space out here—it's an open, airy setting next to Marine Park and right across from Floyd Bennett Field, once an army air field. It is famed as Wrong Way Corrigan's point of departure, and is now used as a training ground for EMS and police drivers, as well as for occasional events (the most important of which, for our purposes, is the annual Native American

Indian Powwow, see page 78). Just across the causeway is another excellent reason to come out here—the **Gateway National Recreation Area**, a great windswept expanse of marsh and beaches, stretching from Breezy Point to Far Rockaway. **Jacob Riis Beach** is the best: it has white sand with large shells, dilapidated WPA-era buildings where you can take a shower or buy something to eat; and a companionable, if well-worn, feel.

Gateway Sports Center, 3200 Flatbush Ave. 718-253-6816

There are other enticing locales for **miniature golf**. One is the **Nellie Bly Amusement Park** in Brooklyn (see page 25, 27) and another is the **Turtle Cove Golf Complex,** located on City Island (this also has batting cages and a driving range). There's also a riverside course at Pier 25 on Manhattan's West Side. (see pagr 111)

Turtle Cove Golf Complex, 1 City Island Rd., Bx. 718-885-2646

Chelsea Piers: Despite its overwhelming publicity blitz, which would make many cool parents wary, this place can be a nice experience for you and your kids. Sky Rink's two indoor skating rinks are spacious, clean, and light-filled, with big windows looking out over the Hudson. Of course, you can sign the children up for all kinds of classes and leagues, but if you just want to give them something pleasantly active to do for an afternoon, with no strings, you have several options: open basketball games (pay by the hour); batting cages; bowling lanes; two outdoor roller-skating areas; and the driving range (in the golf club), which has kid-size clubs.

Chelsea Piers, 23rd Street and the Hudson River.

For Sky Rink, call 336-6100; for children's programs, 336-6666; for the Golf Club, 336-6400; for general information, 336-6000 or www.chelseapiers.com/

RexPlex:

Skate parks are thin on the ground in New York. There are three in public parks: Millennium Skate Park (Owl's Head, see page 26) in Bay Ridge, Riverside Skate Park in Manhattan, and Mullaly Skate Park in the Bronx. Then there's Chelsea Piers (see page 107), a few smaller establishments, and that's it. But just across the river in New Jersey hulks the mighty RexPlex, all 200,000 square feet of it. And it's conveniently located—right across the street from Ikea! RexPlex has two street courses, a 13-foot vert ramp, a four-foot mini-ramp (that doesn't look so mini), and the largest skateboard pipe in New Jersey. There are plenty of lesser ramps and such for neophytes (along with four artificial turf fields, an arcade, batting cages, and more), but if you still find skating and boarding as terrifying to watch as we do, just take a short walk across the parking lot and cool out amidst the sensibly priced home furnishings.

RexPlex, 1001 Ikea Drive Elizabeth, NJ, 1-877-REXPLEX, www.rexplex.com/

Riverbank State Park:

Riverbank's 28 beautifully landscaped acres sit atop a water treatment plant that is elevated 69 feet above the Hudson River. There's a riverside promenade and a park for picnicking, as well as a covered skating rink (rollerblading in summer, ice skating in winter), basketball courts, tennis courts, a softball field, a performing arts center for special programs, and a restaurant. The Totally Kid Carousel is here (see page 126), along with indoor and outdoor pools, both of which have areas shallow enough for wading. Riverbank is wildly popular, so get there early in the day. Take the 1 train to 145th St. and walk one block downhill.

Riverbank State Park, 679 Riverside Drive, 694-3600,
http://nysparks.state.ny.us/parks/

Rye Playland:
This beautifully maintained, land-marked Art Deco amusement park, with its sturdy old rides, tree-lined walkways, paddleboats on the lake, and tranquil crescent of beach, evokes another, calmer era. The magical boardwalk scenes from *Big* were filmed here. Playland is fun and clean, and the 45 rides are just exciting enough for all ages. (The roller coaster is downright thrilling.) Why not make an evening trip up here one summer weekend? (On Fridays and Saturdays, it's open late.)

To get there, take I-95 north from Manhattan and turn off at the Playland Parkway. The Metro-North train goes from Grand Central to Rye, where you take a 10-minute ride on the No. 76 bus.

Rye Playland, to find out more call 914-813-7010
or visit http://www.ryeplayland.org/

Bird-watching:
Because of its strategic location on migratory flight paths, New York is visited seasonally by everything from herons to hawks and weird little warblers, the mere mention of which get enthusiasts' phone wires humming. At almost any time of year, Urban Park Rangers conduct bird-watching expeditions in parks all over the city. Call (800) 201-PARK to find out more. The real thrill comes in the early spring or fall when masses and masses of birds are on the move. Then, take your young naturalist to the **Ramble in Central Park**, 37 acres of woods and streams that the birds consider a very desirable location (after all, it's Manhattan), and the **Jamaica Bay Wildlife Refuge**, which is part of the Gateway National Recreation Area (see 107). Even if you don't have a car, you can reach this enormous stretch of marsh, dune, and water by subway and foot. Here's how:

Put on walking shoes, pack binoculars (and snacks and a picnic), and take the A train to Far Rockaway. Your stop is Broad Channel. From the subway, walk one block west to Cross Bay Boulevard and then north three-quarters of a mile to the entrance to the refuge. (This distance rules out the tinies.) Tours are free, and last up to two hours; there are picnic tables (but no food) and toilets in the Visitors' Center.

For the Ramble and all city bird-watching call (800) 201-PARK

Jamaica Bay Wildlife Refuge, 718-318-4340, www.nps.gov/gate/pphtml/facilities.html

Brooklyn Indoor Sports Center: Nestled

alongside the Gowanus Expressway, this indoor sports center has a friendly vibe and plenty to do: batting cages, clattering arcade games, and a court which can be used for basketball, soccer (with a smaller ball), or field hockey. There's also a party room, a card and memorabilia shop (with many affordably priced items in among the collectibles), and a snack bar called the Dugout that serves all major food groups: pizza, burgers, gyros, even decent coffee. The court is a very busy place and reservations are necessary, especially on weekends. The Sports Center hosts all sorts of clinics and leagues and it's a wonderful place for a birthday party, thanks in large part

 to the consistently friendly and attentive staff. Unless you drive (parking's a cinch), getting there is a bit of a shlep (R train to 25th St. and Fourth Avenue, then walk 3 blocks), but it's definitely worth it, especially on a cold or rainy day, when youthful high spirits are wreaking havoc on your nerves and infrastructure.

Brooklyn Indoor Sports Center, 800 3rd Ave. (between 27th and 28th Streets), (718) 965-0004, www.brooklynindoorsportscenter.com

South Cove on skates, and, for the littlest ones, the city's best playground: New York abounds in cool places to go in-line skating, but one of the coolest has to be right along the Hudson from South Cove to Chambers Street. South Cove itself is probably the most atmospheric stretch of waterfront in the city, with its boulders, tall grasses, wooden pilings, cobalt-blue lanterns, and Japanese bridges. North of the World Financial Center and around the Marina, you find yourself on a long esplanade with a special level for cyclists and skaters. Past the ferry docks, there are benches and grassy lawns for picnics, not to mention *The Real World*, a gloriously eccentric group of animal sculptures by Tom Otterness. Pry

the little ones loose from these with the promise of the city's best playground. That would be **Nelson Rockefeller Park**, between Vesey and Murray Streets. This state-of-the-art facility is built to delight and, with its chain-link climbing nets, animal-head fountains, and foot-powered red carousel, it succeeds. North of here, **Hudson River Park** takes shape. Eventually, the five miles of park will edge the West side of Manhattan from 59th St. clear to the Battery. Right now, there's beach volleyball (real sand!), miniature golf, and a playground at Pier 25; Pier 26 is an ecology center that offers some kid-friendly programs and events.

For information about **Hudson River Park** programs and projects, call 414-9384 or visit www.hudsonriverpark.org

For information about **Battery Park City** progams and projects, call 417-2000 or visit www.batteryparkcity.org

Chapter Six

Pay for Play: Ten Treats that are Fun for Kids, Easy for Parents

1. *Playspace*

New York's first indoor playground is still around, providing a gentle, creative environment for children six and under. The emphasis is on untechnologized play: crawling, sliding, jumping, playing dress-up. There are also classes, free concerts, and one of our town's premier birthday rooms. There's even a decent cup of coffee to be had in the tidy café. Consult Playspace's excellent website for particulars and a closer look at the physical plant.

> *Playspace,* 2473 Broadway at 92nd St. 769-2300,
> www.playspaceny.com

2. *The New Victory Theatre*

The New Victory has always been ahead of its time. Built in 1900, it was first a legit playhouse, then Broadway's first burlesque theater, and later its first triple-X cinema. Now it's the Great White Way's first full-time children's theater, a reliable venue for non-patronizing, quality entertainment by theater companies from all over the world, including Australia's sweetly anarchic Circus Oz and Louisville's distinguished Stage One. Most productions are geared toward kids seven and up.

> *The New Victory Theatre,* 209 W. 42nd St bet. 7th
> and 8th Aves., 382-4020, www.newvictory.org/

3. *The Museum of Television & Radio*

Look, nobody's perfect. It's OK, really, if sometimes you want to just sit placidly with your kids and stare at reruns of old TV shows. Call them "classic" if it makes you feel better. And at the high-tech Museum of Television & Radio they do have classics, everything from "The Ed Sullivan Show" (hey, wanna see the Beatles's first appearance?) to "The Lone Ranger" and "I Love Lucy." You can call up four selections on the computer and then watch them on a console for up to two hours.

> *The Museum of Televison & Radio,* 25 W. 52nd St.
> bet. Fifth and Sixth Aves. 621-6600 or 621-6800 for tape.

Call for details and to find out about special showings for children or visit www.mtr.org/.

4. Baubles, Bangles, Bargains

Take your budding Mizrahi or Karan notion shopping at the **Cinderella Flower and Feather Co.** (60 W. 38th St. bet. Fifth and Sixth Aves. 840-0644), the **Fabric Warehouse** (406 Broadway), and **Gampel Supply** (11 W. 37th St bet. Fifth and Sixth Aves., 398-9222) for beads and such. And, as a weekend way of life, take them to your local flea market, where some will rummage among the ancient purses, vests, or posters while others can pick up a tiny tank or old comic for $1. They're New Yorkers, after all, so they must learn these things.

5. Tours for sports fans—Yankee Stadium and Madison Square Garden
(and while you're about it, why not scream yourselves hoarse at a New York Liberty game?)

A wonderful combination of techie stuff (How do they keep the grass so nice? Where does the ice for the **Madison Square Garden** Christmas show come from?) and reverent moments (in the steps of the Babe! of Clyde!) these one-hour tours are the berries. The Babe Ruth tour at **Yankee Stadium** takes you to the field, the dugout, the press box, the clubhouse, and Monument Park with its busts and plaques commemorating The Great Ones. At MSG, you'll see locker rooms for the Knicks, Rangers, and Liberty, go backstage at the theater, and learn all the technical tidbits involved in maintaining a multi-purpose arena. And there's always the hope that you'll see athletes or performers warming up. At the time of writing, the biggest thrill at MSG has to be watching the **WNBA's Liberty**. Go along in mid-June through August and you'll find yourself immediately swept up in a cult so large and enthusiastic that it's more like a religion.

Yankee Stadium tours, daily at noon. Price: $12 for adults, $6 for children 14 and under. No reservations necessary. For groups of 12 or more, call 718-579-4531. http://newyork.yankees.mlb.com/NASApp/mlb/nyy/ballpark/nyy_ballpark_history.jsp

Madison Square Garden tours, daily, various times. Price: $15 per person, $16 over the winter holidays. For tickets, call Ticketmaster or go to the MSG website, www.thegarden.com

Liberty tickets can be bought through the MSG website, www.thegarden.com or www.wnba.com

6. The Petrel

She's only 70 feet long, but she's fast and beautiful and she sails around the Harbor or up the Hudson from Battery Park, May through September. This is not the Circle Line, this is actual sailing (without having to do any of the work). For details call: 825-1976.

7. Tea at the Plaza Hotel

Go only if your daughter is absolutely obsessed with Eloise, that wonderful book about a spirited little girl who lives and runs wild in the hotel. Why only then? Because it costs $27 per person. For that, you sit in the Palm Court, nibbling little sandwiches, scones and pastries, tea and coffee (and maybe your request for a soda will be indulged), accompanied by the tasteful sounds of a pianist and violinist. If all this sounds enticing, see if you can dig out that nice flowered dress and a pair of shiny Mary Janes for her, some discreet pearls for Mom, and get on over there.

The Plaza Hotel is at 768 Fifth Ave. at Central Park S. 759-3000.

8. Astro Gallery of Gems

This is the city's best place for rocks and minerals, and it also has wonderful jewelry, shells, and African sculptures. For beginners, there's a $5 and $10 rock tray laden with quartz crystals, hunks of amethyst, and polished tumblestones like tiger's eye, obsidian, and fool's gold. Fossil fans will love the belemites ($10–$15), flat polished stones with markings of small wormy things that died long, long ago. You can buy a geode—those mysterious, jeweled caves-inside-stones—for as little as $15. The staff is long-suffering and helpful.

Astro Gallery of Gems, 185 Madison Ave. at 34th St., 889-9000, www.astrogallery.com/

9. Tram to Roosevelt Island and back, followed by Serendipity 3

You've gone by it and speculated about it. What are you waiting for? The tram departs from Second Avenue and 60th Street every 15 minutes, and at the other end you're in a quiet little place that's so unlike the city, you feel it doesn't deserve its 212 area code. The excitingly ruined hospitals and asylums are, alas, all fenced off; so walk north and find an open space for sitting or picnicking, or one of the numerous playgrounds for your youngest. Then, back on the tram, and make straight for the campy, eccentric charm of Serendipity 3, to remind yourself what New York is all about. Sit elbow-to-elbow with movie stars and their kids, tourists, and birthday celebrants. Go for the dishes that have stood the test of time: the foot-long hot dogs, frozen hot chocolate, and the divine Miss Milton's lovely fudge pie. Go crazy and buy a T-shirt, too.

Roosevelt Island Tramway, 832-4543, www.rioc.com/transportation.html

Serendipity 3, 225 E. 60th St. bet. Second and Third Aves. 838-3531.

10. Barnes & Noble

Not only are these stores all over town, they're well-disposed towards children. Storytimes, pajama party–storytimes, author appearances, and special events abound. Browse, buy some pretty paperbacks, and then slump companionably over muffins in the cafe—if you can get in without tripping over all the strollers, that is. www.barnesandnoble.com

Chapter Seven

Downtime: Ten All-time Great New York Movies that You Will Be Able to Watch Happily, at Least for the First Few Times, with Your Kids

---

NOTE: As of this writing, all of these films are available on video. Some of them (i.e. *Searching for Bobby Fischer*) may be over the heads of smaller children. Then again, maybe not. As cool parents, you know what is or isn't appropriate fare for your family.

1. *The World of Henry Orient:*

A Brooklyn con artist turned foreign-born concert pianist and the two preadolescent girls who worship him. Peter Sellers is inspired as Henry, Tippy Walker is delightful as the more troubled of the two girls, and Angela Lansbury is an excellent villainess. Central Park in winter has never looked lovelier.

2. *Superman:*

Christopher Reeves's bow as the legend refurbished for the big screen. Farewell baggy tights and dopey flying effects, hello Margot Kidder and a raft of terrific character actors, including Gene Hackman and Valerie Perrine, whose hideout is located in the bowels of Grand Central Station.

3. *Tootsie:*

Dustin Hoffman's finest hour as a starving actor who becomes a soap opera diva. As sweet as it is hilarious, this gender-bender also features fine contributions from Bill Murray, Teri Garr, Jessica Lange, Dabney Coleman, and Charles Durning.

4. King Kong: The world's most soulful ape has dignity even when hanging off the Empire State Building. And Fay Wray can really scream! Has a special relevance in these days of kids' bath soap in shapes of endangered species.

5. Guys and Dolls: Frank before sainthood, Marlon before statehood, Times Square before porn or gentrification. Purists may carp that Marlon's playing Frank's role and can't sing, but it still has the finest score of all American musicals, along with a wonderful supporting cast (Viva Vivian Blaine and Stubby Kaye!), great sets and costumes, and foist-class Noo Yawk accents.

6. West Side Story: If only juvenile delinquency were really this way. This urban Romeo and Juliet has the power to squeeze tears from anyone old enough to follow the plot—recommended for ten and up. The exteriors were shot where Lincoln Center stands today.

7. Searching for Bobby Fischer: Based on a true story, this movie about an American chess prodigy who gets his start among the patzers of Washington Square makes the ancient game seem as cool as hoops.

8. *Miracle on 34th Street:* Santa Claus comes to town and finds it full of skeptics. This Christmas fable tempers its sentimentality with a nice dose of city wit, but cool parents and kids alike will melt as Edmund Gwenn makes everyone's Chistmas dreams come true. Younger children will fade during some of the romantic longuers. Catch the shots of Macy's Thankgiving Day Parade before television, commercialism, and balloon technology transformed it; here, it might as well be a small-town parade. Even though this is shown endlessly on TV during the holidays, rent it; it's much, much better without commercials. And make sure it's the 1947 original, not the appalling remake with Richard Attenborough.

9. *On the Town:* The patter's a little sluggish and the musical numbers overlong by today's standards, but the opening ("New York, New York") is heaven, the location shots of Manhattan in the fifties are fascinating (catch Columbus Circle pre-Coliseum). As for Frank, Gene, Ann (Miller), Betty (Garrett), and Jules (Munshin)— they're a helluva cast.

10. *A Tree Grows in Brooklyn:* Elia Kazan's first film displays his always extraordinary work with actors. A four-hankie weeper set in Williamsburg, Brooklyn, around the turn of the century, this story of a loving family and its tribulations is best

for older children, who will love the views of children at play in a bygone New York (especially the Christmas tree scene). The brilliant child actress Peggy Ann Garner will steal your heart.

Honorable mention: Ghostbusters may be too scary for the tinies, but they've got raucous New York atmosphere, slimed landmarks, and a walking Statue of Liberty.

Chapter Eight

Ten Places to Visit
and Things to Do for
Which No Parent Should
Ever Be Too Cool

1. Don't be too cool to join the tourists at the Radio City Music Hall Christmas Show.

Why? Because it's there. Despite its maudlin religiosity, the $5 mega-Cokes, and the incessant drone of outlanders, this show really is the last of its kind—a gaudy spectacle of wooden soldiers, live animals, religious tableaux, and the resonant blast of the mighty Wurlitzer. If you should be fortunate enough to witness a live camel obeying the call of nature during the incredibly discreet manger scene, your children will be grateful to you forever. For you, there are the Rockettes, still alive and kicking. Afterwards, zip around the corner and take in the skyscraping Rockefeller Center Christmas tree, another classic, astounding New York sight left too long to the tourists.

Radio City Music Hall Christmas Spectacular, call 247-4777.

2. Don't be too cool to ride on a carousel.

Carousels are one of the few rides children and their parents can sincerely enjoy together. They're safe and easy, they make everyone smile, and they go surprisingly fast; so you should never pass up a chance to climb onto one. Central Park's (65th Street at mid-park, 879-0244) is often so full of courting couples you'd think children weren't allowed on, but they are. Riverbank's Totally Kid Carousel (145th Street on the Hudson, 694-3600) is the city's most idiosyncratic, the mounts based on drawings done by local children. Bryant Park's is the most centrally located and, although it's only been in place since the summer of 2002, looks gloriously turn-of-the-century. Prospect Park's (just south of the zoo, 718-965-8999) is a showcase for the restorers who've brought it back. There are two in Queens, one of them in Flushing Meadows at

111th Street and 54th Avenue (718-592-6539), another in Forest Park at Woodhaven Boulevard and Park Lane (718-805-5572). And don't forget the B&B in Coney Island (see page 87); it's enclosed and a little dingy, but it has a real brass ring to grab for.

3. Don't be too cool to take a round-trip ride on the Staten Island Ferry.

Sure, it's a cliché, and it was more fun when you could drive on. Still, the Staten Island Ferry (foot of Whitehall Street next to Battery Park; 718-815-BOAT) offers one of the only world-class bargains to which New York can still lay claim. Every half hour or so (call for schedules), a ferry pulls away from its docking bay; half an hour or so later, it reaches its destination. The ride is free. Along the way, you've smelled the sea and felt its spray, cruised right by the Statue of Liberty, and experienced no seasickness. The boats themselves look old, battered, and wonderful, with vintage linoleum in patterns that haven't been made for 30 years and wooden benches worn dark and smooth. The food is nothing special, but the hot dogs taste absolutely wonderful at sea, with breezes blowing and engines churning loudly in the background. In fact, munching as you gaze at the Manhattan skyline or Lady Liberty, you'll swear they're the best hot dogs you've ever had in your life.

4. Don't be too cool to experience the Bronx Zoo (except that now it's the International Wildlife Conservation Park).

Don't make the mistake of bringing the kids here when they're too young to appreciate it. All too often Dad ends up with someone on his shoulders who doesn't give a damn about the life-cycle of the

slow loris. How old is old enough for the zoo? A word to the wise: Don't go until your kids are so big they'd be embarrassed to have you carry them. At that age, they can enjoy the World of Darkness, with its swooping bats, glittering-eye lemurs and bush babies, and, weirdest of all, the subterranean colony of naked mole rats. They can take the Bengali Express monorail and see the wild animals they've dreamed of—elephants, tigers, rhinos. They'll love the African plains with their lions, cheetahs, and zebras. For children weary of New York's other "Wildlife Centers," where prairie dogs and sheep and otters stand in for big game, this is the real thing. The Bronx Zoo is like no other zoo in the world. The International Wildlife Conservation Park, Fordham Rd./Bronx River Parkway 718-220-5100, www.wcs.org/home/zoos/bronxzoo

5. Don't be too cool to visit the American Museum of Natural History.

True, New York children go here every year on class trips, and the dinosaur collection is always mobbed, but there are just too many wonders in this vast place for you not to make it a family destination. In the new Discovery Room, a "museum-within-a-museum" aimed at 5- to 12-year-olds, kids can piece together a prehistoric reptile's skeleton or track an earthquake. As always, the tableaux of prehistoric and abo-riginal peoples and the old-fashioned dioramas, with their painted backdrops and taxidermied creatures, are irresistible. The blue whale, hanging from the ceiling as gracefully as a storm cloud, is astounding. The littlest children will race around the polished floor beneath it while you stare, pondering its enormity. If you've the energy, move on to the Rose Center for Earth and Space. Be warned: It's gorgeous and very high-tech, but some of its exhibits can be a little puzzling for young minds, not to mention most mature ones. You can't miss, though, with the Hayden Planetarium show, *The Search for Life: Are We Alone?* With it spectacular visualizations and animations based on the latest data from the furthest space and deepest ocean, this film makes science as exciting as science fiction. How fitting that it's narrated by Harrison Ford, Han Solo himself. The 20-minute show is well worth the supplementary charge over basic museum admission, but you must book before you get there (tickets are available on a walk-up basis, but leave them to the out-of-towners; you don't need another wait on line). At the door you'll get a cool "Passport to the Universe," with a nifty hologram. Hang on to it; it'll help you remember whether the Milky Way is part of the Virgo Supercluster or vice versa. The Big Bang Theatre is a lot of sound and fury, with Jodie Foster narrating the origin of the universe. Kids love to touch the massive and mysterious Willamette Comet in the Hall of the Universe; the nearby crater-making machine gets a lot of play too. Best Planetarium gift-shop gimcrack: a marble-sized globe, with continents of semi-precious stones inlaid in a lapis lazuli sea. Hungry yet? The museum's food court is large and varied, but we prefer heading over to E. J.'s Luncheonette, kid-friendly home of the crisp fry, the thick shake, and the sassy wait-staff.

American Museum of Natural History,

Central Park at W. 79th St. 769-5100, www.amnh.org. Tickets for the Space Show at the new Hayden Planetarium can be purchased online, or by calling 212-769-5200.

E. J.'s Luncheonette, 447 Amsterdam Avenue
bet. 81st and 82nd Sts, 873-3444

6. Don't be too cool to go to the top of the Empire State Building.

Probably you went up it as a child. It's time to go again, soon, and make it a habit. Try going at dusk or on a summer night, or even on a foggy day when the tips of the surrounding buildings poke through the cottony cloud cover. It's just scary enough for the kids to realize how high up they are; the mere fact of taking three elevators up to the top is impressive. Unfortunately, the wonderfully odd and decrepit Guinness World Records Exhibit Hall (the museum that time forgot) has closed down. Don't try to compensate for this loss by taking the Skyride, a jolting, 25-minute "big-screen flight simulator" tour of New York. It will make your younger children queasy and give you the feeling that you've been had.

P.S. Before leaving, linger in the entrance lobby for the wonderful relief image of the building on the wall, and especially for the (newly cleaned up) diorama of King Kong, camera in hand, climbing the tower.

Empire State Building, 350 5th Ave., 736-3100, /www.esbnyc.com/

7. Don't be too cool to climb all the stairs to the top of the Statue of Liberty.

The statue itself is closed indefinitely, but it'll reopen one day and when it does, it's worth the inconveniences—the heat, the crowds, the lines—to go inside. Just allow a lot of time and take bottled water and sunhats if it's summer (waiting for the boat can be a pitiless process). Once there, trek all 354 steps to the top. It

takes awhile, and you should be prepared for some vertiginous moments as you get close to the crown and you're wedged together with all the other climbers on the vertical plane. (So you should save this trip until you feel your children can handle it without getting trembly.) It's mysterious, thrilling, and awesome to be inside that dark, cavernous exoskeleton. The gift shop is a must—you'll be giggly and lightheaded enough after your adventure to pose for pics in those dopey green foam-rubber crowns.

Take the Circle Line–Statue of Liberty Ferry from the Battery, 269-5755. For hours of operation and prices call Liberty Island, 363-3200 or visit /www.nps.gov/stli/. NOTE: Your ferry ticket to the Lady includes passage to Ellis Island, which is newly refurbished and profoundly affecting. Its impact, however, depends on understanding what went on there; so we strongly recommend that you take your children there only when they are old enough—third-graders at least—to know something of the island's history and its meaning to Americans.

8. Don't be too cool to go bowling.

Time was when bowling was the fastest-growing family sport in the U.S., and bowling alleys sprouted all over the city the way microbreweries do today. Those days are gone. Only three bowling alleys remain in Manhattan: AMF Chelsea Piers Bowl, with 40 state-of-the-art lanes, Bowlmor Lanes in Greenwich Village, a groovy '30s artifact, and the Leisure Time Bowling and Recreation Center, in the Port Authority, which also has a small arcade with air hockey and video games, plenty of fast food and drink, leagues of all sorts, and the occasional celebrity bowling event. All have the all-important gutter-closing bumpers that are essential for children and all do birthday parties.

Outside Manhattan, bowling venues abound. For our money, the Gil Hodges Lanes in far-off Marine Park, Brooklyn, is a treat worth the trip: a spacious, state-of-the-art establishment whose gutter-blockers appear at the yank of a lever by one of the lads who operate the joint. There are 64 lanes, baseball memorabilia on the walls (Gil Hodges himself founded the place), and a centrally located bar next to a well-lit and perfectly decent food service (nachos, fries, and dogs are the order of the day). Parking is a cinch; or take the D train to Avenue U, then the B3 bus to Mill Avenue; turn right, walk one block, turn right again on Strickland, and there you are.

AMF Chelsea Piers Bowl, W. 23rd St. and W. Side Highway, 835-2695, www.chelseapiers.com/

Bowlmor Lanes, 110 University Place, 255-8188, http://www.bowlmor.com

Leisure Time Bowling and Recreation Center, 625 Eighth Ave. (at Port Authority Bus Terminal), 268-6909, leisuretime.citysearch.com/1.html

Gil Hodges Lanes, 6161 Strickland Ave., Brooklyn 718-763-3333

9. Don't be too cool to go on a day trip to the beach.

The city beaches are funky, let's face it. Even at Jacob Riis Beach, which is the best maintained, you'll find yourself at awfully close quarters with other people's music, children, and private lives. So

get up very early one day and take yourselves off to Jones Beach. It too can be crowded; but it's a state park, with dunes, surf, and miles and miles of beach. It's an easy trip from Penn Station, and all you have to do once you arrive at Jones Beach Station is trot down the stairs and into the bus. In 10 minutes or so, you'll have sand between your toes. There are optimistic buildings from the thirties; there's everything you need in terms of food, drink, and bathrooms. Remember, early is definitely best here; so that by the time the crowds are heaviest and the sun is at its most relentless, you'll be ready to go home.

Jones Beach State Park, 516-785-1600. For train schedules and prices, call the Long Island Railroad at 718-217-5477.

10. Don't be too cool to take that long-postponed trip to the Liberty Science Center.

True, the Liberty Science Center is not strictly (or even loosely) speaking in New York. So what? The Cool Parents' tent is a big tent. And this place is *close*; an airy, spacious setting with views of the skyline and the harbor, and enough kid-friendly (and even adult-painless) things to see and do to make it worth a family trip.

A caveat for the first-time visitor: Liberty Science Center is so close to the city that you may think you can drive there in a flash. HA! It's quite likely that you will sit in tedious, soul-destroying traffic in the tunnel, where the light is depressing, the air is foul, and there's no radio reception (if you must drive, bring tapes). In no time, you'll be wondering where everything started going wrong in your life and the children will be getting motion-sickness. If you find this prospect daunting, and you should, grab the ferry from downtown Manhattan (see 134).

Once arrived, start with exhibits and save the IMAX movie and the other presentations for when the kids run out of steam; work your way down from the top floor. Everybody will get a kick out of the computerized door frame that announces your height when you stand in it. The exotic live insects are amazing: hefty millipedes the size of snakes, Giant Prickly Stick Insects that look like moving branches, Central American cave cockroaches that will make you grateful you don't hang out in any Central American caves and, of course, an enormous, brown, furry tarantula. Eeeewwww. Decompress in the Estuary/Atmosphere area, where the warty sea robin tooling around in its tank is as scary as it gets. Downstairs, there's virtual basketball, a "perception maze" full of funhouse mirrors and optical illusions, and a Formula One car. Don't miss the liquid nitrogen demonstration; the frozen balloons and rubber balls go over big.

You'll find basic food in The Laser Light Cafe. The gift shop is huge and offers, in addition to standards like astronaut ice cream, skull-shaped maracas, and the once-rare-but-fast-getting-as-common-as-dirt punching skeleton puppets. Why is the Liberty Science Center selling skull maracas? It's exactly the kind of thing you'll obsess about if you have to drive back in traffic.

The Liberty Science Center is located in Liberty State Park, at exit 14B off the New Jersey Turnpike. Call 201-200-1000 or visit http://www.lsc.org/ for information. To get there without a car, take a ferry from the World Financial Center to Colgate Center (daily). From there take the Hudson-Bergen Light Rail to Liberty State Park. Or take the PATH train to Pavonia/Newport and transfer to the Hudson-Bergen Light Rail. For ferries call NY Waterway at 1-800-53-FERRY; for buses, 201-432-8046. You can also take an express bus straight there from the Port Authority Bus Terminal at Eighth Avenue and 40th Street; call 971-9054 for details.

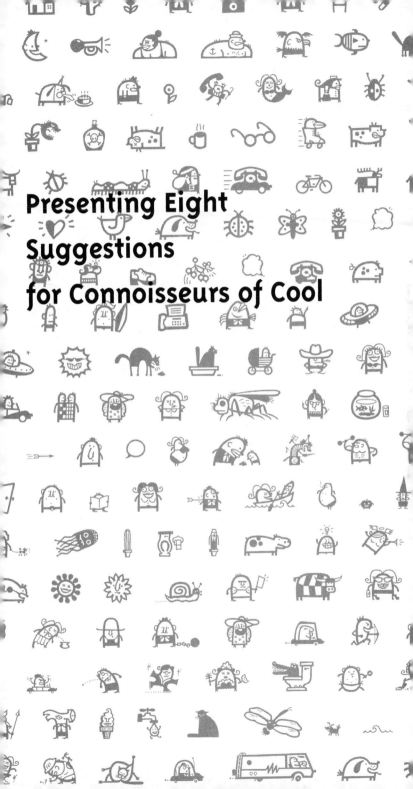

Presenting Eight
Suggestions
for Connoisseurs of Cool

As a cool parent, it's exciting to discover some great new place to see, some new thing to do—even though it's embarrassing when you discover the great place to see or thing to do has been here all along without you even noticing. In a city as protean as New York, it happens. Here are a few recent discoveries:

NYPD True
The Police Academy Museum contains the
world's largest collection of police apparatus and memorabilia, much of it absolutely irresistible to kids: handcuffs, helmets, Al Capone's terrifying Tommy gun, and police vehicles—a cruiser, a scooter, a motorcycle—that you can get in or onto. Learn how to spot a counterfeit bill, stand in a line-up next to a life-size carica-ture of Capone, take your own fingerprints and look at enlarge-ments of Pretty Boy Floyd's after he'd tried to obliterate them with acid. The small but inviting gift shop sells authentic (and really loud) police whistles. Don't forget to take in the building itself. This minia-ture Renaissance Revival palazzo, built in 1911, was originally the First Precinct headquarters. It's considered New York's first modern police station. They really don't build 'em like they used to.

> **New York City Police Museum**, 100 Old Ship bet. Water and South Sts., 480-3100, www.nycpolicemuseum.org
> **Getting there:** 2 or 3 to Wall St., 4 or 5 to Bowling Green, or N, R to Whitehall/South Ferry

The Buzz-a-Rama Experience
Brooklyn kids-in-the-know have made the trek to this dingy, thrilling establishment in Kensington since the dawn of the '60s. Slot-car racing involves a 155-foot swooping, curving, silver track with grooved lanes (or slots) and seven-inch racing cars which hur-tle down the track, steered by your children, at speeds of up to 100 miles an hour. In 1966, there were 40 such places in New York. **Buzz-a-Rama** is the last, and its quietly fanatical owner,

Frank "Buzz" Perri is not planning to close it any time soon. For birthday parties and special occasions, Perri can be persuaded to plug in his spectacular collection of pinball machines.

Buzz-a-Rama 500, 69 Church Ave. at Dahill Rd., Brooklyn, 718-853-1800. Open only on summer weekends.

Getting there: Take the F train to Church Ave.

Red Hook Revelry

Red Hook, the last remaining vestige of Brooklyn's wild and woolly waterfront, is resurgent, bustling with artists and other cool people who've come there to live and work at the water's edge. And, as so often happens, where there are hipsters, you'll find nifty activities for children. Parked at the bottom of Conover Street, the **Waterfront Museum and Show Barge**, otherwise known as The Barge, is the hub of much of this, with its Circus Sundays series. Sitting in its little performance space, bobbing slightly with the movement of the waves, you get up close to jugglers and clowns, and stare out at the Statue of Liberty just across the water—it's low-key, friendly, charming. **Dancing in the Streets**, a citywide performance group, also presents memorable site-specific events (involving a mix of dance and theater and, often, oral history) that resonate in Red Hook's stark, compelling landscape. Finally, you'll all get a kick out of the **Brooklyn Waterfront Artists Coalition (BWAC) Annual Pier Show**. On a weekend in early summer, trek down to the **Beard Street Pier** and step inside the ancient, cavernous, and darkly atmospheric warehouse that houses the BWAC show. The art is always innovative and often downright weird—in other words, fascinating to the younger set. Outside, there's food, drink, roaming hipsters, and, if you go on the opening weekend, dancing to a live band on the cobblestone street. What could be better? As for souvenirs, be sure to pick up one of the deeply cool BWAC T-shirts—a new design each year. Finally, take a quick stroll down Coffey St. (between Conover and Ferris Sts.), with its neatly maintained old houses, for a glimpse of Red Hook's past.

> **The Waterfront Museum and Show Barge**,
> 290 Conover St. (at Pier 45), Brooklyn, 718-624-4719,
> www.waterfrontmuseum.org
>
> **Dancing in the Streets**, www.dancinginthestreets.org
> **Brooklyn Waterfront Artists Coalition**
> **Annual Pier Show,** 499 Van Brunt St., Brooklyn,
> 718-596-2507, www.bwac.org/
>
> **Getting there:** Take the A, C, or F to Jay St./Borough Hall,
> then the B61 bus to Conover St., or the F or G to Smith-9th Sts.,
> then the B77 bus. Free Con Edison Shuttle bus from
> Brownstone Brooklyn to Circus Sundays.

Divine Pastime

Begun in 1892, the **Cathedral of St. John the Divine** is still unfinished; when it is, it'll be the biggest cathedral in the world, combining Gothic majesty with New York references in a way that tickles kids. After gaping up at the towering nave and the Rose Window, go outside and look at the stone carvings on the building's west front. Next to Biblical figures, you'll find images of the city carved by city kids, contemporary stonemasons who've been trained by English craftsmen. Each Saturday, the cathedral presents workshops in the medieval arts for young children. Sculpt a clay gargoyle, chisel away at a block of stone, make your own illuminated letter using tracing paper and real gold leaf, do a brass rubbing, weave at two looms (and take home a small cardboard loom of your own) and, finally, create a stained glass collage with tissue paper. This is a great workshop in an incredibly atmospheric location—and if it's a hit, you can book it for a birthday.

> **The Cathedral of St. John the Divine**, 1047 Amsterdam
> Ave., bet. Cathedral Parkway and W. 113th St.,

932-7347, www.stjohndivine.org/
Getting there: Take the 1 or 9 to 110th St., or the B or C
to Cathedral Parkway

Glass Act
UrbanGlass is a find—a glassblowing center that welcomes
children. Located in a cavernous loftlike space in downtown
Brooklyn (think: easy to get to), it hosts various family programs.
Show up for one and you'll start by watching work in progress. It's
seriously hot here, with three glowing furnaces and sweaty artists
hoisting globs of molten glass in and out of them. When the kids
tire of watching, they can paint on glass (which then gets fired) or
create their own sandblasted piece of art. Just bring a glass cup or
jar along and the instructors will provide stickers for decoration.
The decorated items are put into a sandblasting oven and literally
bombarded with sand particles. When they emerge, they have a
chic, opaque finish—all except for the parts covered by the stickers.
Peel off the stickers and you'll find clear glass underneath. The
result is quite impressive. Older kids might be sufficiently excited by
this hot yet cool environment to enroll in a glassblowing class, or at
least the paperweight workshop.

> **UrbanGlass,** 647 Fulton St. (entrance at 57 Rockwell St.),
> Brooklyn, 718-625-3685, www.urbanglass.com/
> **Getting there:** D, M, N, Q, or R to DeKalb Ave.

Abracadabra, etc.
Tannen's Magic Studio is the largest magic shop in
the world (8,000+ tricks in stock), and professionals are always in
evidence, shopping and kibitzing. Still, beginners of all ages are welcome. The salespeople are all magicians and will happily demonstrate tricks—but only once (customers who figure out tricks tend
not to buy them). Magic sets for 5- to 8-year-olds can cost up to $30,
but you can spend much less. Spooky the Ghost Handkerchief, for

instance, sells for $8.50. Private lessons and classes are available, and there's a week-long magic camp in August.

> **Tannen's Magic Studio,** 24 W. 25th St. bet. Broadway and Sixth Ave., 929-4500.
>
> **Getting there:** F, N, or R to 23rd St.

More than Just a Stage

Theatreworks USA is a long-established company which presents well-conceived, handsomely staged children's theater based on folk tales, historical subjects, and books such as *Swiss Family Robinson* and *Oliver Twist*. The hour-long original productions are, more often than not, substantial and satisfying—real theater that speaks to children. From October to April, the company's base is the Promenade Theatre, which doesn't seem to have a bad seat. Babies are not permitted, and if your kids get loud or restless, you can watch the show on a monitor in the lobby. Buy a season subscription and your tickets will be much cheaper.

> **Theatreworks USA**, Promenade Theatre, 2162 Broadway cor. W. 76th St., 647-1100, www.theatreworksusa.org
>
> **Getting there:** Take the 2,3,1, or 9 train to 72nd St.

Dance that's Doable

Several times a year, the **Joyce Theatre** presents an hour-long family matinee. The dancing is uncompromisingly professional and rigorous, but the approach is always crisp, lighthearted, and appealing, and the selection of pieces so skillfully done that even the smallest children become absorbed. Afterwards, there's a question-and-answer session and autograph opportunities for the youngest balletomanes. If you become a member, there are big savings and other benefits.

> **The Joyce Theatre**, 175 Eighth Ave. cor. W. 19th St., 242-0800, www.joyce.org
>
> **Getting there:** Take the C or E train to 23rd St.

INDEX

Festivals

About the Authors

Between them, Alfred Gingold and Helen Rogan have published eight books, including *Items from Our Catalog* (Gingold), *Mixed Company: Women in the Modern Army* (Rogan), and *Brooklyn's Best: Sightseeing, Shopping, Eating, and Happy Wandering in the Borough of Kings* (together). They've written for *New York Woman*, the *New York Times*, *Life*, *Time*, and many other publications. They live in Brooklyn with their son.